D0757932

Make It Happen!

Live Out Your Personal Brand

Justin Honaman

iUniverse, Inc.

New York   Bloomington

Make It Happen!
Live Out Your Personal Brand

Copyright © 2008 by Justin Honaman

iUniverse books may be ordered through booksellers or by contacting:

iUniverse
1663 Liberty Drive
Bloomington, IN 47403
www.iuniverse.com
1-800-Authors (1-800-288-4677)

ISBN: 978-0-595-53079-3 (pbk)
ISBN: 978-0-595-51816-6 (cloth)
ISBN: 978-0-595-63135-3 (ebk)

Printed in the United States of America

For mom, dad and Garman. The absolute best family for which a son and brother could ever ask. I am forever thankful!!

A portion of the proceeds from the sale of this book will go to the USO (United Service Organizations). Learn more about the USO at WWW.USO.ORG

Contents

To laugh often and much; to win the respect of intelligent people and the affection of children; to earn the appreciation of honest critics and endure the betrayal of false friends; to appreciate beauty, to find the best in others; to leave the world a bit better, whether by a healthy child, a garden patch or a redeemed social condition; to know even one life has breathed easier because you lived. This is to have succeeded.

- Ralph Waldo Emerson

Introduction

Ten years ago I walked across the stage at Alexander Memorial Coliseum on the Georgia Tech campus accepting my Bachelor of Industrial Engineering degree from Dr. Wayne Clough, our president. My mind was a blur of excited thoughts and questions: How did five years of college go by so fast? What was I getting myself into just two weeks later at Ernst & Young as a consultant in the Process Improvement consulting practice? Where would I be in ten years and what steps would I take to get there? What would define me as a person and leader?

I had many questions but few answers. In hindsight I can see how every moment since that day at graduation has formed me into the man who sits in front of this keyboard typing out his thoughts. I look back over incredible business experiences, intense relationships and many life lessons learned for just this moment. The decisions made then affected my career path, how people related to me privately and professionally, and communicated what I valued most. How people perceive me is based on what

I offer them as a human being; they relate their experience with Justin Honaman to how I treat them and the amount of trust I build with them. All these thoughts are blasting through my brain at warp speed when … it hits me.

I realized that every person is like Starbucks, Coca-Cola, Chick-fil-A, Nike or Nordstrom — companies that represent trust, quality, and service. But these aren't just companies, they are brands. They are specific, recognizable identities that we all experience daily and with whom we build a kind of relationship. I know that sounds weird but it's true. I continue to frequent Starbucks because I not only love their coffee, but I love the experience and options at their stores. I shop Nordstrom because of their unbelievable customer service and attention to detail. They desire a relationship with me. Not a one-time sale. You get the picture. So my thought is this; if I am the "Justin Honaman" brand, what defines me? How do people feel when they experience me? What brings them back for more? What do they associate with me — arrogant jerk, or fun-loving, business-minded, singer-songwriter, make-things-happen guy? I hope the latter!

So here I sit thinking about my last ten years since college graduation and wondering how these years have shaped the Justin Honaman brand. Here's what I've come up with.

The following pages hold my insights, advice and revelations on how to form a personal brand that will stand the test of time — a brand that may help you to make a real difference in the lives of others. A brand that is consistent – and positive. Do you get it? Good! Let's get started!

CHAPTER 1

The "Your Name Here" Brand

"I like talkin' about you, you, you, you usually, But occasionally, I wanna talk about me!"
— Toby Keith, *I Wanna Talk About Me*

ME-MAP!

You are given a clean sheet of white flip chart paper, fifteen minutes and multi-colored, fruit-smelling permanent markers. Your assignment: draw a "Me-Map" or "snapshot" of your life. Tell your story — no words, only pictures. Paint a picture of what is important to you. Upon completion, you will present yourself to a group of 30 new friends — people that you have never met before today. Go!

What would you draw? What images immediately come to mind? What pictures tell your life story? How would this single page communicate who you are – your family, your education, your work, your activities and interests?

If you have ever taken part in this icebreaker, you know that the results are different for each individual. Some individuals use

1

massive pictures, all the colors in the marker set, and positive images, while others use the black and blue pens, and are more structured in their depiction using simple themes, bullets and fine print. Once each individual has presented their story, and all of the flip chart pages are posted on a wall, the wall speaks of many different individual stories collectively representing varied backgrounds, experiences and interests. Immediately you notice similarities and unique qualities of each individual. Each page reveals the author's singular life-print and offers a glimpse into their experiences. Their story. Their brand.

Your Personal Brand, Defined

Before we go further with this whole "personal brand" idea let's define our terms. What is a brand[1]? From a corporate perspective, a brand is a company's face to the world — a company's name, and how that name is visually expressed through a logo, and how that name and logo extend throughout an organization's communications. It also relates to how customers perceive a company — the associations and inherent value they place on the business. A brand is a kind of promise; a set of fundamental principles as understood by anyone who encounters a company. A brand communicates an organization's identity and dictates how that identity is communicated to key audiences, including customers, shareholders, employees and analysts. Finally, a brand represents the desired attributes of a company's products,

---

[1] www.persuasivebrands.com, www.wikipedia.org

services, and initiatives. Ok, enough of the corporate lingo — time to make it personal.

Your personal brand consists of many things: knowledge, experiences, personality, friends, family, accomplishments, failures, values, relationships, faith and much more. What is the value of your personal brand? How do you live out your personal brand at work? In your home? In the community? With friends and family? What components of your brand are strong — what are weak? What is your personal look of success?

In this book, we will focus on five *core relationship focus areas* for use in defining your personal brand:

- Self
- Work / Career
- Family
- Faith
- Community

Each of these focus areas work together to support your personal brand as depicted in the *Live It Out (LIO)* personal brand model. At times, dynamic tension may exist between focus areas of your personal brand. This tension forces the prioritization of your personal and professional activities while strengthening the framework of your personal brand.

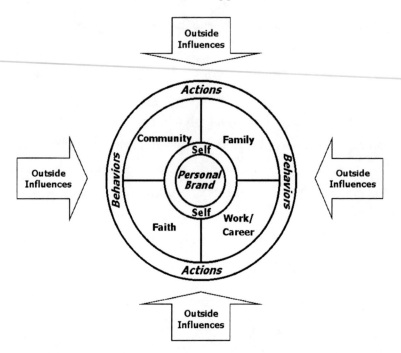

Your brand is as strong or weak as the performance in these five areas. The value of your personal brand increases or decreases over time based on actions taken within each area.

The foundation of the *Live It Out* model is your "Self" component. This includes your personal values, ethics, morals, behavior traits, personality, knowledge, creative talents, and other inherent skills and abilities. Faith, Family, Community and Work / Career are the "variable" personal brand focus areas that work for me but these may be different for you (we will cover this later in the book). Each relationship focus area is linked to the "Self" component.

As you determine your focus areas, it is important to realize that relationships are of critical importance. Think about the relationships that define your life: faith-based relationships, work relationships, community or philanthropic organization relationships and family relationships. These relationships are interwoven into the context and lessons conveyed in the following chapters.

Think of your personal brand as a bank account. The value of that account increases when you invest in relationships with your family, when you complete a new training program, receive a new degree, or even when you lead a volunteer program for a community organization. It increases when you develop a stronger relationship with God. It increases when you spend time learning from your parents, siblings and extended family. It increases when you commit time and / or money to philanthropic programs. And most importantly, it increases when you gain a better understanding of your personal values, ethics, morals and beliefs — your authentic self — and live them out in your everyday personal and professional interactions.

Alternatively, you deplete the bank account as you make decisions that take away from the five focus areas. When you demonstrate negative actions towards colleagues. When you treat a member of your team unprofessionally. When you intentionally hurt a loved one. When you gossip about friends and engage in hypocritical behavior. When you cheat on a spouse. When you lie on expense reports. You get the idea. You are depleting the bank account and crippling your personal brand when you engage in these types of behaviors.

As you progress through the book and identify with the primary life lessons, take time to assess the things that are going well in your life and those areas requiring improvement. Use this text as a guidebook to identify opportunities for change in your life. Take the opportunity to define the different elements of your personal brand. Understand that while this book, and the model inclusive of the Family, Work / Career, Faith and Community components work for me, your focus areas may differ. Let's look at some ways you can begin to define your personal brand. It all starts with your core values.

DEFINE AND UNDERSTAND YOUR CORE VALUES

Meyers Briggs, Self-Perception Test, Resiliency Test, DISC profile, Learning Styles Inventory … you have probably heard of one of these, if not all, and have most likely completed one. The essence of these tests is to define your core values. They reveal what's inside of you and how your core values manifest themselves in both personal and professional situations.

All of your "life" decisions are based on your core values. They are central to your personal brand. Define them. Write them down. Carry them with you. Review them.

Sample Core Values			
Ambition	Stewardship	Integrity	Patience
Competency	Empathy	Service	Respect
Individuality	Accomplishment	Responsibility	Dedication
Equality	Courage	Diversity	Teamwork
Enjoyment	Wisdom	Honesty	Accountability
Loyalty	Independence	Innovativeness	Dignity
Credibility	Security	Excellence	Compassion
Empowerment	Challenge	Efficiency	Focus
Quality	Influence	Learning	Dependability
Collaboration	Friendliness	Discipline	Passionate
Generosity	Persistence	Optimism	Organization
Flexibility	Mentoring	Ownership	Active Listening
Teaching	Consistency	Proactive	Commitment

While all of these may "seem" important, choose five that are most important. Rank order those five. Review your life activities vs. these five core values and assess what's working and where you may need to make changes. Refine your core values over time. Re-evaluate regularly. But don't just settle for writing them down — live by them. Living out your core values strengthens your personal brand. This separates those who strive for excellence and those who are content with mediocrity.

THE DRIVERS BEHIND DECISIONS

When I am faced with major decisions in life, I review my personal brand framework to identify where and how the new opportunity or challenge fits in. My core values are foundational and support many major focus areas that currently include the consumer goods industry, my desire to be a subject-matter-expert (SME) in the area of business intelligence and marketing, my passion for faith and it's role in all aspects of my life, my focus on giving back through work in the community, and my passion for mentoring and coaching others.

At the end of the day, I look for opportunities that enable me to positively impact organizations and individuals with whom I interact, while striving to help others achieve happiness, professional growth and personal success. Simple? No. But this is the way that I think about my life and major decisions. How do you structure your thoughts and ideas around career? Personal life? Decisions? It helps me to write things down so I created the following diagram to remind me of my priorities and to be a tool for use in communicating my business priorities to others in the workplace.

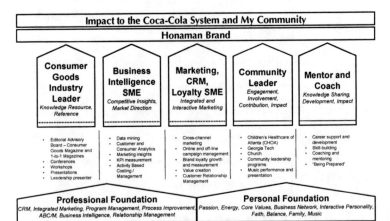

Guiding Principle: Positively impact each organization and individual with whom I interact while striving to help others achieve happiness, professional growth and personal success.

A very good friend of mine, Jany, recently shared with me her approach to managing major life decisions. Jany is a successful financial advisor and has customized a common financial rating tool to help her make informed personal decisions. The Morningstar ratings are a method of rating mutual funds and they include a nine-box grid outlining risk and size of companies covered by the fund. Jany created her own nine-box grid to help her focus when making life decisions, to appreciate the things that really matter, and to spend her time wisely. Her core values, personality and beliefs are the foundation on which all other relationships and successes are built and therefore touch or enable each of the other eight boxes.

She has clearly defined what she views as important in her life. Having it written down and documented helps her to focus and apply herself effectively. These are the things that, for her, define her personal brand. This is important because busy people are constantly asked to join new committees, serve in a leadership capacity on trustee boards, assist with new fundraising efforts, mentor others, teach classes, and the list goes on. It would be easy to take on too much and therefore be ineffective in many of these areas. Jany has found a method of focusing on the things most important to her. This method may not work for anyone other than Jany. The important thing is that she has structured her thinking and approach towards life and her priorities.

Two other business colleagues developed their own working personal brand frameworks to represent their values and interests. These diagrams developed after we defined career and personal objectives together — and how to communicate in pictures (personal brand snapshot) in addition to words (resume). These perspectives are unique and that is the expectation. It's personal — individual. Imagine the story that can be told in an interview — beyond the resume, case examples, and standard strength and weakness questions — when you can share a model of the things most important to you both personally and professionally.

My Personal Brand Perspective
Vision: Multi-cultural, international marketer

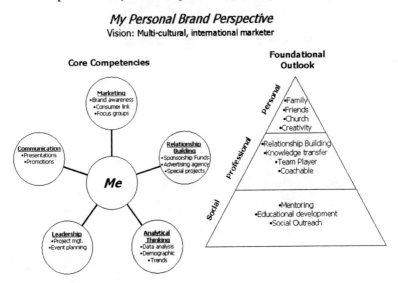

My Personal Brand

**"Strong team player.
Passionate about developing customer relationships.
Focused on execution."**

My professional values • Integrity • Accountability • Teamwork	**My personal values** • Loyalty with personal relationships • Work hard. Play hard. • Education
My strengths • People skills • Effective persuasion • Completing time-critical tasks • Deep knowledge of my org structure	**My passions** • Competitive sports • The Great Outdoors • International travel • Experiencing new cultures
My upbringing gave me a motivating environment which stressed appreciation for hard work and determination to achieve my goals.	**I work well with** a broad-based collaborative team in which each member uniquely contributes to the operational performance.

I challenge you to think about your "message," your focus and how you structure your approach to life. Develop your own diagram — your own way of defining what's important to you. How would you define and outline your core values, priorities, areas for focus, and life decision enablers outside of a resume? By taking the time to think about your life in this way you become more focused. Living with focus and purpose is contagious.

One last thought before we move on. One of my favorite prints hanging at my home is a picture I picked up while consulting for Walt Disney World Parks and Resorts in Florida. It depicts Mickey Mouse looking at himself in a mirror. While looking at himself, he is drawing a picture of what he sees — his drawing is of Walt Disney.

Walt Disney's heart, soul and mind are what make up Mickey Mouse. There really is something amazing and special about Walt Disney. I don't know of many individuals, regardless of age, that do not feel like they are in a truly special place when at a Disney Park. As one of my very best friends stated, "There's just something about the experience. I feel young again. I remember being there with my family. I forget about everything else going on in the world. I relax and live."

As we move into the next section reflect on this question: If you were drawing your own self-portrait, who or what would be depicted on the canvas? Your parents? Friends? Or something else — something that pictures and words cannot accurately reflect.

> *"The successful person is the individual who forms the habit of doing what the failing person doesn't like to do"*
> — Donald Riggs

CHAPTER 2

Self: Your Personal Brand – Live It Out!

Core Focus Area in Definition of Your Personal Brand

Life Lessons

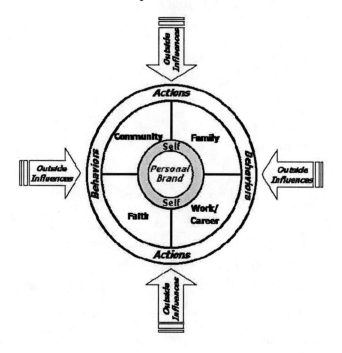

WHO I AM. WHO ARE YOU?

"They said it couldn't be done … but I'm all about makin' it happen, I'm all about gettin' things done, I like to get up early, Work overtime, Do whatever it takes, For God and country my life, I'm all about makin' it happen!"
— Justin Honaman, *Makin' It Happen*

WEEKDAY SCHEDULE

5 a.m.: Wake-up

5:30 a.m.: Workout / swim

7:30 a.m.: Arrive at office

8 a.m.: Kickoff to all-day meetings

7 p.m.: After-work networking event / community or philanthropic activity / family / music / books / writing / favorite TV shows

This, is my life. And I absolutely love it!

I am "that guy" that operates best with many proverbial balls in the air — none of which may be dropped and all of which are made of glass. I am high-octane. Full of energy. I enjoy juggling work, personal, community, spiritual and philanthropic commitments. I am always on the go and never miss a beat. I am driven. Focused on people and results. Passionate. And absolutely cannot stand when someone tells me something is unachievable. I don't fit the mold, I break it. I make things happen.

Why this attitude — this M.O.? I honestly don't know. But what I do know is that I am passionate about making a difference. About giving back. About helping others. About using my talents and skills to better my community and our world. To positively influence others. I thrive on the happiness of others and love when I bring a smile to the face of a stranger. I am passionate about the personal and professional development of those that I have the opportunity to manage. I feed off of the positive energy of others. I am a connector, a mixer — I value relationships. I put my heart into relationships and people. And I wear my emotions on my sleeve. I am the definition of transparent.

I enjoy being the proverbial "worker bee" when others are clamoring to lead meaningless initiatives. I avoid negative energy and the individuals that propagate negative thoughts and ideas. I challenge the way that "things have always been done" and strive for something better — something not mediocre. I am a tiger. A magician. And I will never settle. Ever.

This is me. This is the way I think. My thoughts, actions, attributes, values, experiences, and much more. These make up my personal brand — the Justin Honaman brand. When you're done reading this book, I want you to be able to write out who you are just as I have done. I want you to know what makes you tick, what is central to your core — what defines you.

The following sections offer some field-tested advice on how to build up your "self". Let's start by looking at the importance of pursuing a dream.

Pursue Your Dreams and Passions

"Some people wait a lifetime, for a moment, like this"
— Kelly Clarkson, *A Moment Like This*

"If I had all the money in the world ... " How many times have you heard that phrase? It amazes me that so many people fail to pursue their dreams. Forget about the perceived "small and un-important" passions in life. Ignore individual gifts and talents. They make excuses for why they never followed-up on an idea, a calling, a true love, or that little voice in their head:

"It was so much easier when I was single."

"I have kids and a family now so I have little time
to pursue the things that I truly enjoy — those
things that allow me a total release."

"I am too old to pursue my desires ... at
least that is what society tells me."

Does this sound like you?

Living at home, in high school or college everything seemed possible. There was nothing to worry about — little personal responsibility. But as we get older, life seems to take on added complexity and it forces us out of our "creative" zone and into a "routine" zone. The days become shorter and the hours seem to fly by. There are many priorities and most take precedence over our personal desires, interests or hobbies. We forsake creative talents because of a lack of perceived time and resources.

Whether you recognize it or not, we are all born with personal talents and gifts. Some are small, some are large; some are obvious while others are more subtle. All are significant. Many are ignored or go unused.

Growing up in Florida, I always dreamed of being an astronaut. I attended Space Camp for four years in Huntsville, Alabama, I visited the Kennedy Space Center, and I even worked for NASA for three years while in school at Georgia Tech. I was as close as one could be to going into space as I worked numerous launch operations for NASA. I was living a dream while working Space Shuttle launch and landing operations with an amazing team of dedicated NASA and contractor employees at the Kennedy Space Center. I worked with the NASA leadership in delivering on shuttle team obligations and helped ensure critical flight safety for shuttle missions. Tell me again what is impossible? Sure, it's not space but close!

Here's another more recent example. Two and a half years ago, I decided to follow-up on a "whisper in my ear" to get back into music. Growing up, I sang in the church choir, played piano and performed in a jazz band for a number of years before high school. I found the time, made a small investment in equipment and made it happen. Three months into voice lessons, my voice coach, Heidi Higgins, suggested I start writing songs. "Impossible!" was my first thought. But once I got started, the songs streamed out of my pen faster than the ink could dry. Today, I have written close to 30 songs. Many people laughed at my endeavor and could not believe that I was singing country music and thinking about releasing an album! But that's exactly what I did.

I decided to parlay my musical interests into a country music album and to use the album to raise money for a children's charity (Children's Healthcare of Atlanta). I traveled to Nashville regularly to interview producers and hit it off with my current producer, Bob Bullock. Bob has worked with many top country acts including George Strait and Shania Twain to name a few. And

Bob offered to work with me — "no-name" Justin Honaman! Bob is an incredible producer. He's patient, yet detailed and not afraid to push back to ensure the best possible product. Those that laughed at my idea are the same people that failed to pursue their own personal passions or failed to follow-up on a dream.

What's holding you back? What steps can you take to make time for that one passion, that one hobby or that one interest? You don't want to look back on your life and say, "if only … " Go ahead, follow a dream. You never know where it might lead.

As my good friend Giovanni Livera[2] states in his book Live a Thousand Years, "Anything truly is possible — live the extraordinary life!"

> *"Don't be afraid of the space between your dreams and reality. If you can dream it, you can make it so."*
> — Belva Davis

REFLECT

"Back when a hoe was a hoe, Coke was a Coke, And crack's what you were doing, When you were cracking jokes, Back when a screw was a screw, The wind was all that blew, And when you said I'm down with that, Well it meant you had the flu, I miss back when"
— *Tim* McGraw, *Back When*

How often do you take 30 minutes during the day to reflect? Do you ever take time out, away from the phone, away from email, away from the Blackberry, away from the iPod; time to assess and

---

[2] Giovanni Livera, Giovanni Experiences (www.giovanniexperiences.com)

evaluate? Time to think about your career, about a relationship, or your family? How often do you truly sit back and review what is going on in your life — good and bad — and determine what it might mean? When was the last time you evaluated where things are going and what changes should be made or the impact you are having on the lives of others?

Several years ago, I had the opportunity to go through a skills-based leadership development program. Our kickoff retreat was at Camp Twin Lakes in central Georgia — an incredible camp that hosts children's programs year-round. The camp programs focus on providing an opportunity for children with cancer or other life-threatening illnesses to enjoy the countryside and "camp" activities while they are fighting life-changing circumstances.

We were there during an off week and therefore had a very quiet, secluded period for our retreat. One activity during the retreat was to take time to sit alone and reflect for an entire hour — to spend time with our self — quiet time. We were charged with writing a letter to ourselves outlining priorities, things we would want to change about our lives, things that are important, and any other thoughts that come to mind. It was amazing and completely opposite from my standard on-the-go life.

The first ten minutes that I sat alone on the lake, I thought about work and all the things I needed to do after the retreat. But then, as I had more time to relax, I found that I truly was able to think about my priorities — about what's important in my life: family, friends, relationships at work, time spent volunteering, and my faith. An hour was not enough.

One year later, I received my letter in the mail. It reminded me to make time for myself — to reflect. When was the last time you spent an hour with yourself? Try it. It's not easy but you will reap the benefits in all areas of your life. Remember, don't neglect yourself. If you want to develop a personal brand that has stability and authenticity, then you will need to take the time necessary to keep your core uncluttered. The clearer your mind and soul, the easier it is to avoid a negative attitude and fight off negative sentiments often pervasive in aspects of society today.

POSITIVE ATTITUDE CHANGES EVERYTHING (PACE)

"But all I can do, is all I can do and I keep on tryin', And all I can be is all I can be and I keep on tryin', There's always a mountain in front of me, Seems I'm always climbin' and fallin' and climbin', But I keep on tryin"
— Trace Adkins, *I'm Tryin'*

"Justin, there is nothing YOU can not do with a positive attitude."
— Don Kyser, *Tallahassee YMCA*

I had just completed 10th grade. Upon arriving home from school, my parents sat my sister and me down to share with us that due to my dad's job change, we were going to have to move to Tampa from Tallahassee, Florida. What was initially the most disappointing day of my life, evolved into one of the most significant days of my life. I did not recognize it until several years later.

That summer, I attended a camp in the Blue Ridge mountains. It was called Blue Ridge High School Values conference. It was the most significant week of my life. To this day, 18 years later, I still read the messages, notes and stories I accumulated that week.

What was it about those seven days in the Carolina mountains? That week I met my first true love (her name was Katie). I learned more about myself than ever before in my 16 previous years. I made the transition to a confident extrovert from a shy kid. I learned even more about music. And most importantly, I learned about faith and its role in my life.

That week, I learned that a positive attitude truly changes everything. It can repair a negative or challenging situation. It gives each of us at least a chance to make things happen and is less work than being negative. With a positive attitude, anything is truly possible.

I rolled back into my new hometown of Tampa after that week, as a truly changed person. I understood how to make "I" statements vs. "You" statements. I caught myself when I was sucked into a negative conversation. I avoided people that cultivated an environment of negativity. Perhaps most importantly, I started taking notes of the lessons learned in my life (many of which are documented in this book). I learned from my own mistakes and successes, and those of others.

I think my parents and sister thought I was a bit strange after that week — something was different. To this day, I keep this four-letter word on my white-board, in my Blackberry, and in my notebook:

PACE

Positive Attitude Changes Everything

The lessons I've learned about maintaining a positive attitude can be summed up in a story about a chance meeting with Chan Gailey — one model for PACE.

***

I met Chan Gailey in the Orlando Airport Delta Crown Room. It was his first season on the job as head coach of the Georgia Tech Yellow Jackets. Chan had been an NFL coach for many years and was returning to college athletics to coach "GT". It's always interesting to me to see how people are brought together and on this day, it was Chan and me.

I love college football — especially Georgia Tech football. I grew up in Tallahassee, Florida during the time when Bobby Bowden went from new college football coach on the block to all-time coaching great. My allegiance to FSU changed quickly while a freshman at Georgia Tech. Charlie Ward single-handedly beat Georgia Tech in their first year meeting in the ACC on a last-minute drive. My Garnet and Gold was quickly replaced with Old Gold and White!

Anyway, back to the story. When I saw Chan picking up a Diet Coke in the Crown Room, I could not help but introduce myself to the first year head football coach. We spoke for 15-20 minutes about football, ideas on how to market Georgia Tech athletics, our families and what not, and we said our goodbyes.

We then found our seats next to each other on the flight (no, I did not arrange this!), met our rides together in Atlanta upon landing, planned dinner, and ever since, have remained very good friends.

Chan is 55. I am 34. What's wrong with this picture? Absolutely nothing. During his first years on the job, he was heavily criticized by a small, but vocal group of alumni and friends of the school. I wrote him many notes and emails to let him know that there were many more that were supporting his endeavors at Georgia Tech. He was the perfect fit, and still was through his release from Georgia Tech in November of 2007. Chan completely embodies all that is a leader: focused on character and integrity, committed to building a winning program, and doing right by his players and coaches. I learned a lot from watching Chan handle the ups and downs of college football — winning seasons and losing seasons, amazing performances and embarrassing blowouts. Through it all, Chan was an outstanding leader — someone to look up to and appreciate.

Off the field and out of the locker room, Chan is a true friend and confidant. He is always willing to lend an empathetic ear while sharing wisdom and advice at just the right time. He is never afraid to lay the facts on the table. Chan takes an interest and for that I am thankful.

What was so interesting about watching Chan's career at Georgia Tech was that he consistently managed to avoid the negative rhetoric that surrounds all athletic programs — college and pro. He set a positive example for others to follow. He followed through and was true to his word. There is no doubt that Chan's personal integrity spilled over into his coaching and helped him ward off the negative comments of frustrated alumni and the press.

Chan always surrounded himself with others of great character, positive attitude, and strong leadership. He avoided spending time with the negative people in the world and leveraged a strong foundation of faith to help him navigate difficult times. I learned a lot from Chan and we all can learn from people like him.

Chan loved Georgia Tech. He loved his players. He won consistently year-after-year at a very tough academic institution. And, most importantly, he impacted the lives of many young men and women. Hirings and firings are part of life. We may not always agree with the decisions and yes, we all can learn from these experiences — even when it is others walking the path.

***

I miss Blue Ridge. I miss that week. I miss the experience — the bonfires, singing, rock-slides, free hugs, "way-out games", first kisses, many laughs and just as many tears. I miss the people — new friends that were so accepting. I am so very thankful that I had that week as part of my life. I am sure that if you attended camp growing up, you have similar memories. Life was so easy …

Challenge yourself to an "Attitude Check" daily. You will find that the benefits are realized quickly. Your peers will respond and overall, your stress and worry level will decrease. Consistently maintaining a positive attitude is a challenge. It cuts against the tide of negative sentiment. If you can, model your attitude after someone you respect — someone who lives positively. You'll find that you can learn a great deal by watching the actions of others.

Don't let anyone steal your joy!

A Creed to Live By

Don't undermine your worth by comparing yourself with others,
It is because we are different that each of us is special.
Don't set your goals by what other people deem important.
Only you know what is best for you.
Don't take for granted the things closest to your heart.
Cling to them as you would your life, for without them life is meaningless.
Don't let your life slip through your fingers by living in the past or for the future.
By living your life one day at a time, you live all the days of your life.
Don't give up when you still have something to give.
Nothing is really over until the moment you stop trying.
Don't be afraid to admit that you are less than perfect.
It is this fragile thread that binds us to each other.
Don't be afraid to encounter risks.
It is by taking chance that we learn how to be brave.
Don't shut love out of your life by saying it's impossible to find.
The quickest way to receive love is to give love, the fastest way to lose love
is to hold it too tightly, and the best way to keep love is to give it wings.
Don't dismiss your dreams.
To be without dreams is to be without hope; to be without hope is to be
without purpose.
Don't run through life so fast that you forget not only where you've been
but also where you're going.
Life is not a race, but a journey to be savored each step of the way.
— Nancye Sims

RESPECT AND APPRECIATE OTHERS

"I live for little moments … like that"

— Brad Paisley, *Little Moments*

I have been told many times that you can tell a lot about a person by observing how they treat the service staff at a restaurant. I was not sure I believed it at first but over time, as I attended group dinners with business associates, I started to easily recognize those in the group that were unappreciative. Looked down on others. Treated others poorly and did not even recognize that they were "giving this away" by how they treated the service staff.

It's not just at a restaurant. I have found this also to be true in the travel industry. I truly believe that airline staff, and especially those serving in airports and on daily flights, have one of the most challenging jobs in our country. They have little to no control over factors like weather, over-bookings, fare changes, long security lines, seat mis-assignments, full overhead bins, and stopped up lavatories! If you have traveled at all, I am sure you have witnessed travelers "going off" on a member of the airline staff who, oh by the way, are often not empowered to make a difference in the given situation. Do you want to be one of these people? I am embarrassed for these travelers. Not only do they expend unnecessary energy blowing-up, but they also have just treated someone in a way that they would not want to be treated and on top of that, did so in front of others. We all represent more than just ourselves every single day — we represent our employer, our church, our community organization, our family and our personal brand. Your behavior may reflect poorly on the organizations with which you are associated.

How do you treat those that are in service roles and are working hard to take care of you? Do you treat others the way that you would like them to treat you? How you treat others is a barometer for who you are as a person. Are you over-demanding, impatient or inconsiderate? The next time you feel that "emotion" building-up inside of you, step back, take a deep breath and dial-it down. You exhibit your personal brand in the way you treat others — bottom line.

PERSISTENCE PAYS OFF

"Someday I'm gonna be famous, Do I have talent, well, no, These days you don't really need it, Thanks to reality shows"

—Brad Paisely, *Celebrity*

Persistence + Patience + Positive Attitude = Success!

Who would have ever thought that I would start taking voice lessons, write songs, recruit a top producer, record a country music album, and market it globally? I have had the most amazing time with music and to be honest, it's only just begun!

Not to say that there have not been the naysayers — the negative-nellies. The glass-half-empty folks that tell you something just won't work. The folks that use the "c" word (aka. "can't") way too often. As I was preparing to launch my first country music album, *Saturday in the South!*, I contacted one PR firm (via a friend's referral) to discuss marketing and promoting my album. The first words out of her mouth were, "you're really too old to be doing this and gain any traction." I thought, "Um, excuse me? 31 years old is too old? PLEASE ..."

That was before I sold close to 1,000 copies of my album in less than five months. That was before my first single was being played on more than 120 country music stations in the United States and more than 185 stations in Europe and Australia. That was before I had raised several thousand dollars for an incredible children's charity, Children's Healthcare of Atlanta, through my album sales. Hmm. What did you tell me could not be done? Why should I listen to your negative opinions? As one of my bosses once said, "Opinions are like noses, everybody has one and they all smell!" (Note: there is a more direct version of this saying but I thought not appropriate for this book!)

I have learned a lot about those that tell you something "can't" be done. In my mind, it's really all about who defines and measures success. For example, let's look at my country music album. In my mind, success was recording the first song I had ever written. Success was working with Nashville's top talent to create an amazing finished product. Success was performing in front of people — bringing smiles to their faces and seeing them truly get into something I had written. Success was most importantly selling that first CD so that I could make that first contribution to an amazing children's organization. Success was doing it, when others just talk about it. And success was living out an artistic talent, passion and interest.

Alternatively, one could use industry success measures: #1 single on country music charts, X# million records sold, world tours. Based on these criteria, my project would not be a success.

The point is, do not let others define success for you. Define your own success metrics. Be persistent. Make it happen and stop talking about it before you regret not doing it. Remember, these are things I've learned over the last 10 years that have helped me shape my personal brand. Persistence will differentiate you from the crowd. There are plenty of people who give up or quit — or never even try. Don't be that person. Define a vision. Outline short and long-term achievable goals to get there. Make it happen!

> *"Nothing in the world can take the place of persistence.*
> *Talent will not; nothing is more common*
> *than unsuccessful men with talent.*
> *Genius will not; unrewarded genius is almost a proverb.*
> *Education will not; the world is full of educated derelicts.*
> *Persistence and determination are omnipotent.*
> *The slogan press on has solved and always will*
> *solve the problems of the human race.*
> *No person was ever honored for what he received.*
> *Honor has been the reward for what he gave."*
> — (John) Calvin Coolidge

No Shoes, No Shirt, No Problems

"No shoes, no shirt, no problems, Blues what blues ... Hey I forgot em', The sun and the sand, And a drink in my hand, With no bottom, No shoes, no shirt, no problems"
— Kenny Chesney, *No Shoes, No Shirt, No Problems*

It is by far one of my favorite "thoughts to live by" concepts — don't sweat the small stuff. Even the book by the same title is one of my favorites. To me, this translates into, "why worry?" I fundamentally do not worry. I don't use that word nor do I allow those feelings to enter my daily life or routine. I do get concerned about things, at times, but do not worry.

It is one of the attributes that I see in many individuals and my response to it is simple. In a week, a month, six months, a year, will you still be concerned that this event took place? Or that you made a mistake? Or that you didn't pursue a new opportunity? Is the "small stuff" important in the here-and-now or is it something truly to be concerned about? I guess it's my way of maintaining some level of perspective. Life is more than one small or large issue.

Some individuals are eternal worriers. They are not happy unless they are worried about some aspect of life — a relationship, situation at work, family issue, today's traffic. For me, I have found comfort in letting things roll off my shoulders. I attempt to focus on what I can impact or control — what I can change or do something about. I don't have the time for the "worry" stress. I am a person that believes in God's plan for my life; a plan that I can't modify or change yet still feel confident in its existence.

One of my good friends, Michael, who is in commercial real estate, was telling me about a trip he recently took for business. His stops included a number of Asian and Middle Eastern countries. Traveling through impoverished and low-income neighborhoods, he witnessed children playing, laughing and enjoying life. In thinking through what he saw, his key takeaway was, "Knowledge, fame, and wealth do not matter in the grand scheme of things — they don't equal happiness." He is right.

I have traveled to many other countries and found places where the smallest things are the most important to its people. We often do not appreciate the many blessings in life. Are you worrying about things you can't control? How do you handle the short-term issues and concerns in life? Worry can negatively impact your personal brand. It will keep you from chasing your dreams with confidence. It will keep you on the ropes wondering "if only" instead of forging ahead. It will prevent you from living out your many talents, skills and abilities.

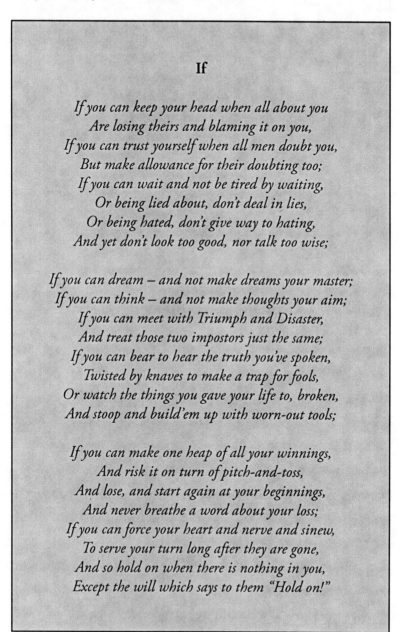

If

If you can keep your head when all about you
Are losing theirs and blaming it on you,
If you can trust yourself when all men doubt you,
But make allowance for their doubting too;
If you can wait and not be tired by waiting,
Or being lied about, don't deal in lies,
Or being hated, don't give way to hating,
And yet don't look too good, nor talk too wise;

If you can dream – and not make dreams your master;
If you can think – and not make thoughts your aim;
If you can meet with Triumph and Disaster,
And treat those two impostors just the same;
If you can bear to hear the truth you've spoken,
Twisted by knaves to make a trap for fools,
Or watch the things you gave your life to, broken,
And stoop and build 'em up with worn-out tools;

If you can make one heap of all your winnings,
And risk it on turn of pitch-and-toss,
And lose, and start again at your beginnings,
And never breathe a word about your loss;
If you can force your heart and nerve and sinew,
To serve your turn long after they are gone,
And so hold on when there is nothing in you,
Except the will which says to them "Hold on!"

> *If you can talk with crowds and keep your virtue,*
> *Or walk with kings — nor lose the common touch,*
> *If neither foes nor loving friends can hurt you,*
> *If all men count with you, but none too much;*
> *If you can fill the unforgiving minute,*
> *With sixty seconds' worth of distance run,*
> *Yours is the earth and everything that's in it,*
> *And — which is more — you'll be a Man, my son!*
>
> — Rudyard Kipling

TAKE CHARGE OF "DEMOLITION DAY"

"I know something's broken, Cause I just started smokin', And shakin', and chokin', Like my old truck"
— Tim McGraw, *Something's Broken*

Starting over is never easy. Sometimes it's necessary and not always by choice: divorce, loss of a job, death of a family member, the end of a family relationship. Just like deep cleaning a house, it is necessary to make a mess before things get better and can be better. Sometimes it is necessary to tear things down to the foundation, and re-build an even better, stronger "home." One that has a new foundation, new building blocks and with the right angles; one with the nooks and crannies that give it character. It's never easy and it takes time.

I am not proud nor am I regretful of the fact that I have been married and divorced. I would never have thought that I would be "that guy" that went through a divorce. One of the most difficult days of my life was the day that my ex and I decided to dissolve our marriage and move on, separately, and in different directions. We made this decision based on many factors and, together, learned a lot from our experience. I am fortunate that she is still an incredible friend. It was not easy making the decision but at the end of the day, it was the right decision for us both. It was a "demolition day" for our relationship. We both have moved on and I can honestly say I am a better person because of my experiences with her.

All of us, at some point in our lives, are forced to make difficult decisions that involve a "re-start" or demolition of some practice and starting anew. For some, it might be a new job or career — leaving an unethical, unfriendly or unprofessional environment. For another it could be quitting work to stay home with a new child; taking the one opportunity to impact a new life from the outset. It could be a decision to move to a new city — to get out of a rut, crazy traffic and the proverbial rat race. It could be ending an unhealthy relationship. It could be eliminating a bad habit — like smoking, drinking, drugs or reliance on medication. Or it could even be trusting God for the first time.

If you need a "demolition day," make it happen and start living a new life with a new base, a new foundation, on which to build. Starting over can be your first step towards establishing the "new you" brand.

> *"Let's do it! Let's make it happen!!"*
> — Ty Pennington, *Extreme Makeover: Home Edition*

UNDERSTAND DIVERSITY

"There's something wrong with the world today, I don't know what it is, Something's wrong with our eyes, Seein' things in a different way, God knows it ain't His, It sure ain't no surprise, We're living on the edge"
— Aerosmith, *Livin' On The Edge*

Several years ago, I was selected to the class of one of the top leadership development programs in Atlanta. I was humbled yet excited about the opportunity. Upon meeting the other class members, I was truly impressed. Not only were they making things happen in the community, they were also interested in making themselves better through relationships and partnership. They were diverse — they represented non-profit firms, blue chip companies, entrepreneurial organizations, law firms, and more.

My new friends were also diverse in race, religion, political interest, personal relationship preference, education, and business experience. This was, to me, one of the most important, yet unexpected, parts of the program. At age 32, I learned more about other races and cultures than perhaps any other time in my life.

Diversity is such an interesting topic and one that most people rush to avoid in conversations and discussions. I now realize why. Most people are not informed on the topic. Diversity is often forced down the throats of managers at large firms thereby further driving a wedge between individuals of different races and cultures. Diversity and inclusion goals and metrics are commonplace at most public companies and typically do not include programs centered on education and awareness. Therefore, managers and staff become fixated on recruiting targets and employee metrics instead of truly understanding the value of diversity in the workplace and how to manifest an environment that is open to people from differing backgrounds.

Many people that we work with, walk past, and ride with daily, are dealing with internal struggles related to the way they are treated due to the color of their skin, the strength of their political views, their sexual preference, their family upbringing, or their lifestyle and behavior.

There is no doubt that for most people, the diversity discussion can be uncomfortable. But it is critical for leaders to comprehend. It is important for leaders to be able to recognize the strengths of others, and conversely, those areas that are unintended, societal weaknesses. We need to realize that while a colleague may outwardly be happy, internally they may be dealing with strife brought on by factors that to many, are not overtly obvious.

As I was completing this book, I was watching an episode from *Extreme Makeover : Home Edition* and one of the statements made during the program jumped out at me. This statement was made by an amazing young man that is blind. "I see blindness not as a disability but more as an ability. Some people with sight tend to judge others by what they see on the outside. I see people for who they are on the inside. Color of skin does not matter to me because I can't see it." Sounds simple. Why do we make it so complex?

SELF-MONITOR

"The drinkin' bone's connected to the party bone, The party bone's connected to the staying out all night long, And she won't think it's funny and I'll wind up all alone, And the lonely bone's connected to the drinkin' bone!"

— Tracy Byrd, *Drinkin' Bone*

Authentic leaders are self-aware. They take care to watch how they come across to their customers and are consistently seeking to improve in their areas of weakness. Do you self-monitor?

Walk into any Barnes & Noble and you will find a myriad of books on leadership: qualities of a leader, steps to become a leader, managers training to be a leader, seven habits and so on and so forth. One thing that I have learned is that long-term success is more likely when you check your ego at the door. When you are attentive to your actions and behaviors. When you manage your emotional highs and lows.

Self-monitoring is the process by which each one of us actively manages our thoughts, ideas, communication and actions enabling a more effective style of communication and activity.

I often think of self-monitoring as personal "filtering." During interactions with others, I actively manage what I am saying, how I am saying it, my body language, style, and words. At the same time, I work hard to interpret the feedback provided through words and body language of others. I evaluate the response vs. my expectations of response. I am also cautious to share only what is necessary with certain individuals while providing more detail and personal insight to others based on our level of mutual trust.

The filter gets better over time and with practice and observation of others. This concept can be learned but only with desire and personal buy-in or commitment. It's as simple as watching others, taking notes on what works and does not work, then working to implement the approach. Most often, the self-monitoring trait develops over time through coaching, feedback and experience.

Self-monitoring is also being aware of others' perception of you and your actions. Let's consider several examples. It's your first month on a new job and you get wasted at the company Christmas party. Big deal? Maybe not. Perhaps the perception of others at the party was that everyone should have too many drinks and need to take a cab home from the yearly Christmas party! And perhaps new hires are expected to go over-the-top in drinking and cavorting at the event. My guess is that most companies are not like this. I call this action a career-limiting move — one that others do not forget.

Or perhaps you enjoy hitting on, asking out and / or checking out married women / men when you are married yourself. What example does that set for others? What are the long-term consequences personally ... and professionally? Do you think before you act?

Self-monitoring requires you to first recognize that this concept is a priority. Then, take action to implement a framework on which you can manage your life decisions. Your actions and behaviors directly reflect your personal brand. Try it — strengthen your personal brand and stop making career-limiting moves, embarrassing statements, or life-altering actions today.

EXERCISE YOUR MIND AND BODY

"Yeah, Runnin' down a dream, Never would come to me, Workin' on a mystery, Goin' wherever it leads, Runnin' down a dream!"
— Tom Petty, *Runnin' Down a Dream*

Another facet of building up your brand is self-discipline. I mean this as it relates to the cultivation of your body and mind. How many books did you read last year? How often do you get out for a run or brisk walk? Do you exercise daily? Or not at all? What key concepts did you learn through training programs, conferences or other events in the last quarter? Do you believe in lifelong learning?

Education does not stop in high school or college or in grad school. Every day is filled with new learning opportunities: in the classroom, on the streets, or in the boardroom.

Exercise your mind. Read, read, read, read, read and read more. If not books, then magazines or newspapers — even online publications. Just make sure you're reading. Why? Reading adds context to life. It provides you with a greater sense of our world and the challenges faced outside of your personal "box".

Recently, I met with an incredible leader that has been a part of the Coca-Cola System for many years. He is a very successful business executive, community leader and key contributor to the long-term success of the company. One of his primary messages to me was to read and accept any opportunity to speak and present to others. He reads a book a week and makes time to fulfill public speaking engagements on a regular basis. His theory is that one has the opportunity to influence others through knowledge shared in public speaking and communication. His advice was succinct and to the point.

I have many favorite books. One that I use with my teams regularly is *Good to Great* by Jim Collins. The concepts are applicable to businesses of all sizes and many companies use this book to help drive paradigm shift within corporate cultures. I assure you that through the 4-5 key concepts in Jim's books, your assessment of leadership within your organization will change. By leveraging the concepts, you can make changes that will flow against the political tide. Jim's books are examples of written material that can have a direct impact on your life, career, and / or business. If you don't already, begin to enhance and shape the "you"-brand with great reading — you won't regret it.

Some of my favorite leadership and personal development books include those listed below. Each provides perspective, insights and ideas that may or may not work with your style of leadership and learning. For me, they work – and this is just a short-list of my favorites!

***Good to Great**, Jim Collins*
***The Five Dysfunctions of a Team**, Patrick Lencioni*
***Built to Last**, Jim Collins*
***The 80/20 Principle**, Richard Koch*
***Courageous Leadership**, Bill Hybels*
***Seven Habits of Highly Effective People**, Stephen R. Covey*
***The Leadership Challenge**, James M. Kouzes, Barry Z. Posner*
***The Fifth Discipline**, Peter M. Senge*
***Failing Forward**, John Maxwell*
***Radical Leap**, Steve Farber*
***The 21 Irrefutable Laws of Leadership**, John Maxwell*
***Love Is The Killer App**, Tim Sanders*
***Lincoln on Leadership**, Donald Phillips*

The body fuels the mind — or so it's been said. So, exercise your body. Make time for physical exercise. I swim and work out regularly at my gym during the week. My goals are 45 minutes of cardio and 45 minutes of "all other" at least five days per week. This time affords me an escape from my Blackberry, emails, text messages and conference calls. It also gives me time to think — and of course, burn calories.

Exercise is critical to your health. There's no excuse for not finding the time. We all have family, friends, long plane flights, extended hours, heavy dinners, strong drinks, and other "top priorities." Find time. It is truly the fuel for physical and mental performance. I developed the ideas for more than half of my songs while swimming and exercising. Take small steps (no pun intended!) and you will benefit.

SIMPLIFY

"Don't worry, About a thing, Cause every little thing, Gonna be alright!"
— Bob Marley and the Wailers, *Three Little Birds*

Do any of these words or phrases define your daily or weekly life: Busy, non-stop, on-the go, back-to-back, meeting mania, many balls in the air, 20-hour days, work is my life? Or do you find your life simple, balanced and comfortably managed? Do you have time to get things done? Do you get the right things done the right way? Do you spend time doing things that you enjoy? Do your "things" — your cell phone, Blackberry, laptop, iPod, Xbox, wireless network, Bluetooth earpiece — make your life more or less complicated? How many balls are you able to juggle effectively, without dropping the one(s) that are truly important?

THE DASH

I read of a man who stood to speak, at the funeral of a friend.
He referred to the dates on her tombstone, from the beginning ... to the end.

He noted that first came the date of her birth, and spoke of the
following date with tears,
but he said what mattered most of all, was the dash between those years.

For that dash represents all the time, that she spent alive on earth ...
and now only those who loved her, know what that little line is worth.

For it matters not, how much we own; the cars ... the house ... the cash ...
What matters is how we live and love, and how we spend our dash.

So think about this long and hard...are there things you'd like to change?
For you never know how much time is left. (You could be at "dash
mid-range.")

If we could just slow down enough, to consider what's true and real,
and always try to understand, the way other people feel.

And be less quick to anger, and show appreciation more
and love the people in our lives, like we've never loved before.

If we treat each other with respect, and more often wear a smile...
remembering that this special dash, might only last a little while.

So, when your eulogy's being read, with your life's actions to rehash...
would you be proud of the things they say, about how you spent your dash?

— Linda M. Ellis ©1999

Take time out to assess during a given week. Outline what activities you accomplish over the period of seven days. What were the results? Were you more or less content after completing the week's activities — delivering results and moving on to the next "thing."

At times, we must make difficult decisions regarding where to spend our time. These decisions are founded on life priorities and often may be difficult to fulfill. For most people, it seems like time moves faster and faster as we age and yet, the requests of our time continue to increase as we attain greater knowledge, wisdom and experience.

As I mentioned earlier in the book, I am a person that operates best with many balls in the air. I am more efficient with more going on vs. less. This works for me and I must constantly manage the ongoing time commitments. Still, I find ways to simplify.

Take control of your life, your time, your engagements, and prioritize. Narrow the focus. Make the difficult decisions, where needed, to simplify. Enjoy the results and appreciate that you are more effective as you truly focus on doing the right things for you. Understanding the idea of simplification will further solidify your personal brand in that you will be known for what you do best — no frills, just one transparent you.

First Impressions Can Make or Break

"Ladies and gentlemen please, Would you bring your attention to me, … Like nothing you've ever seen before, Watch closely as I open this door, Your jaws will be on the floor, After this you'll be begging for more."
— Saliva, *Ladies and Gentlemen*

First impressions are huge. As the old saying goes, "you never have a second chance, to make a lasting first impression." Situations like a job interview, meeting the parents for the first time, attending your first board meeting, your first day of college, a first date or even visiting a church for the first time are all great examples of "the first impression."

The list goes on and is lengthy. First impressions are a first and lasting indicator of an individual, an organization, a group or a community environment. You, as an individual, offer a first impression each time you meet a new person, walk into a job interview at a new company, or engage with a new community organization.

How important are these impressions? First impressions are how many managers make hiring decisions. First impressions are how parents initially evaluate you — the "significant other!" If you read books and magazine articles on the subject, you will find that the first few minutes of an interview are when hiring decisions are often made. What you wear and how you present yourself, your initial comments, and more are how many people assess your skills, abilities, interests, confidence and personality. Tough, but true. The way that you present yourself in these and many other situations is important. Most employers expect you to make an effort and when you are lazy, it is obvious. And the same is true for personal relationships.

At my church, our Host team, which includes greeters and ushers, operates at all times under the catch-phrase "Lasting First Impressions." In a "seeker-friendly" church environment, this is absolutely critical. Any person attending a service or function for the first time, is most likely to meet a member of our Host team first, before meeting any other members or guests. The church and environments within the church are set up to ensure that at no time, should a guest be confused, lost or unsure of where to go, what to do, how to get involved, etc. Our greeters must be outwardly observant and focused at all times. And our ushers must be actively managing the crowd — finding seats as needed, helping the disabled, setting a positive environment prior to guest arrival, and welcoming others with a friendly face and simple "Hello."

Do you make a lasting first impression? What makes it memorable?

Key Points

> ➢ **Pursue Your Dreams and Passions**
>
> ➢ **Reflect**
>
> ➢ **Positive Attitude Changes Everything (PACE)**
>
> ➢ **Respect and Appreciate Others**
>
> ➢ **Persistence Pays Off**
>
> ➢ **No Shoes, No Shirt, No Problems**
>
> ➢ **Take Charge of Demolition Day**
>
> ➢ **Understand Diversity**
>
> ➢ **Self-Monitor**
>
> ➢ **Exercise Your Mind and Body**
>
> ➢ **Simplify**
>
> ➢ **First Impressions Can Make or Break**

CHAPTER 3

Family: What Life is About!

Core Focus Area in Definition of Your Personal Brand

Life Lessons

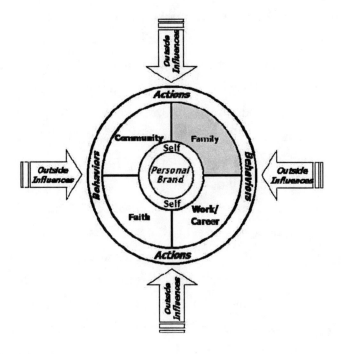

MAKE TIME TO VISIT AND LEARN FROM YOUR FAMILY

"Hey, that's what it's all about, Hey, this is a life I couldn't live without, No I couldn't live without, It's a moment frozen there in time, When the reasons all begin to rhyme, Love's a little bigger, And you finally start figuring out, That's what it's all about."
— Brooks & Dunn, *That's What It's All About*

What do you know about your mom, dad, aunt or uncle? Besides their birthday and anniversary date, what do you truly know about their lives? How did they grow up? What unique experiences and worldly events took place when they were younger; before you were in the picture? We often take time with our family for granted and regret that we did not make time when it was available.

I have been very fortunate. I grew up in a family with strong principles and values. My parents met through a singles group in Pensacola, Florida called the "Swingles!" My mother stayed home with me and my sister. She did not work and was always there to pick us up from school, take us to piano lessons, choir, swim practices and all of the other extra-curricular activities in which we were involved. Homework was first priority before any TV. And there was no such thing as Xbox (although we did have an Atari game system!). We had to eat our vegetables and on occasion could actually have dessert (but this was not the norm!). I can vividly remember gagging on coleslaw — yuk! This family / home foundation was very important to my sister and me. Without it, I know we would not be where we both are today; in our personal and professional lives.

Quick sidebar ... I believe that my sister and I are who we are because my mom was a stay-at-home mom until we were in school. It made a difference that she managed us as kids during the day growing up while my dad worked. My mom started work in development and fundraising at the junior level in Tallahassee, Florida *after* my sister and I were in school regularly. Her career has progressed continually and today, at 64 years old, I can honestly say that she absolutely loves her work. Her career is truly peaking. And she adds immense value to her organization. She makes a difference. Why? I could offer any number of guesses but my gut says faith, attitude, values and focus are somewhere in the mix!

Back to the story ... through middle and high school, my parents were always there for basketball games, swim meets, graduations, piano recitals, choral performances, were chaperones for dances, and much more. We took many family vacations together and I learned so much about the world outside my hometown.

Leaving "home" for college was one of the most difficult, and yet best, things I ever did in my life. It was important as I gained an even stronger sense of personal responsibility and accountability and at the same time, appreciated my parents and "home" that much more.

Family is mom, dad, brothers and sisters. Our family still gets together regularly for Sunday dinners and it's always interesting to see what territory we are going to cover in a given week. For example, my father flew Med-Evac helicopters in Vietnam. He has amazing stories from his years of flying in the Army. It seems like no matter how many times we talk about it, there's yet another story, another hero, another experience that we had not covered in previous conversations. I was born in 1973 and would not truly understand the Vietnam War were it not for my father. It is a significant part of his life and one that he enjoys sharing — he absolutely lights up when a friend asks him about his military experience (or anything associated with leadership). I even wrote my first song, *Shadow of the Blade*, based on my dad's flying experience over Vietnam (this song will be a cornerstone for my next album). In addition, I made the decision to donate proceeds from this book to the USO (United Service Organizations) as a tribute to the actions taken by those serving for all of us in the U.S. military.

Family is *more than* mom, dad, brothers and sisters. I recognize that many individuals are from broken families. From families that do not value strong relationships. And from families where spending time together is not a priority. Family may be defined as much more than just mom and dad. Family can be close friends, colleagues, partners and relationships who you define as "family."

One of my favorite television shows is *Extreme Makeover: Home Edition*. I love it for many reasons and one of the episodes even inspired me to write a song called *The Healing Tree*. One message that I find consistently conveyed by the families in the show, is that life can be much shorter than one might expect. God has a plan for each of our lives and for some, tomorrow, next week, next month, a good friend or family member could be moving on. Have you shared your feelings with your family or close friends?

Family is grandmothers, grandfathers, uncles, aunts and cousins. One person I miss greatly is my grandmother. I never will forget her babysitting me as a child. Attending my wedding. Playing Bunco on a Friday night. It was so difficult and surreal being with her as she took her final breath. To be there by her side. She taught me many great life lessons and her interest in caring for others was unbelievable. It's funny how an experience like that makes you truly focus on the "right" things in life.

Family is loving relationships. "If you are in love with someone, they always look the same regardless of age over time," stated my good friend Jack over dinner one night. We were discussing relationships and he offered this simple idea. One thing I have found is that I truly appreciate feeling that sense of caring, safety, relationship-confidence, and love that comes from a true bond. Life can many times be about work, and status, and meetings, and parties, and everything else. But a significant other and associated love and devotion, take things to a different level. It's no fun growing old alone. I miss love dearly when I do not give it or receive it often enough. And I would hate to let my life go by without making family a priority.

Life is short. You never know what tomorrow will bring. Take time to visit with and learn from your family. Remember, your personal brand does not exist apart from your family. No regrets.

EXPERIENCE THE WORLD TOGETHER

"Reading departure signs in some big airport, Reminds me of the places I've been, Visions of good times that brought so much pleasure, Makes me want to go back again, If it suddenly ended tomorrow, I could somehow adjust to the fall, Good times and riches and son of a bitches, I've seen more than I can recall ... "
— Jimmy Buffett, *Changes in Attitudes, Changes in Latitudes*

What memories exist in snapshots on the frig? Or in a screensaver on your Macbook? In frames on your desk at work? What do you see when you read departure signs in "some big airport"?! I've never been there? I would love to go there? I wonder what that place is like? I don't have time to take vacation? I can't break away from my job?

Does this sound like you? Take action. Get out of your house or apartment or condo and make time to travel. See the world. And do it with someone you care for. Someone that will enjoy and appreciate the experience with you!

I have found that it is all-too-easy to get caught up in day-to-day / week-to-week routines. No time to take off of work. No time to plan a "big trip" (aka. long weekend ... heaven forbid a week or more!). Not able to get away from clients, customers, partners. Don't know where to go to find the best deals.

I have been all over North America, to Europe and the Caribbean many times. Every time I travel, I give thanks that I made the time and spent the money. I learned something new. I visited a unique place. I learned about an amazing culture. I left the Blackberry at home. I turned on my "out-of-office" email message. I was not reachable. I could think. I could write. I could enjoy learning about another part of the world.

It was not easy. I truly enjoy working. I love lots going on. But I found that I also love learning more about a part of the world I would never otherwise have the opportunity to enjoy. Even a small town in a different part of our amazing country. I also need time to recharge. And I enjoy experiencing new places with someone that I love.

I am so thankful that I have had the opportunity to experience difference cultures in different parts of the world. To have enjoyed the pizza, wine and Italian culture in Rome and Florence. To have snorkeled with sea-horses, squid, parrot fish, and turtles in the South Caribbean. To have bought a Cuckoo Clock from a clock-maker in Heidelberg, Germany. To have experienced a true Belgian waffle in Brussels. To have floated through the canals of Amsterdam (and of course seen the Red Light District!). To have heard the music echo through waterways and pathways of Venice. To understand how important Buddha is in Japan and to have visited a monastery — and oh by the way, watched the Japanese school kids' fascination with my sister's blonde hair on a train in Tokyo. To have driven through the Alps and peered deep into an azure blue lake with sparkling, crystal-clear waters. To have visited a country filled with poverty. To understand that others in the world appreciate so little and yet we expect so much. To have seen 35+ bald eagles fishing, resting and soaring in front of our restaurant in Ketchikan, Alaska. To have sat on the beach next to a resting sea lion in Kauai, Hawaii while appreciating the vast South Pacific full of sea turtles, porpoises and more.

I promise you will not regret it. You will never truly understand another part of the world, another culture, another people, without immersing yourself in that country. That city. That town. Before you tell me or anyone else that it is too expensive and you don't have time, do your homework. Go online. Talk to a travel expert. Go on a mission trip. There are plenty of travel options that will take you to new places. On your timetable. Within your budget. Enjoy your life ... and share your stories. Cover the refrigerator with photos — life memories — and allow those experiences to shape you while strengthening the value of your brand. Again, no regrets!

HAVE PATIENCE

"Have patience, Have patience, Don't be in such a hurry, When you get impatient, You only start to worry, Remember, Remember that God is patient too, And think of all the times when others had to wait for you!"
— Bible School (Frank Hernandez, Sherry Saunders), *Patience*

What thoughts come to mind when reading the following?

- Long, snaking security lines at the airport
- 1+ hours in line to ride Space Mountain at Disney World (even with FastPass!) on a 105 degree day
- A six-hour round of golf
- Traffic into L.A., Chicago, New York or Atlanta between 7-9 a.m. Monday through Friday; or out from 4-6 p.m.
- A slow-poke in the highway left / fast-lane

- Those people in their cars that zoom down the road and cut in line just at the exit during rush hour (some days I wish I had a police badge!)
- Fourteen months from engagement to wedding
- Meeting all of the "wrong" women (or men) and pushing hard to "find" the right one because of age or loneliness
- Weather delays and canceled flights
- Slow or no service at a "top" restaurant
- A promised promotion on-hold due to OPEX reductions
- A career that seems to be stuck in third gear
- Extended deployments of a brother, sister, mother or father in Iraq, Afghanistan and other war zones

These, and many other similar examples, challenge the patience of most individuals. One thing that I have learned is that by expending extra energy getting worked-up or stressed about these situations, the outcome is likely not any different. For example, blowing up at a gate agent due to a canceled flight gets you nowhere. It was not his fault and you have just expended a lot of energy for no reason (and oh by the way, stress is not healthy). Honking while in traffic — pointless. Settling for the wrong person for the wrong reasons — set up for divorce and / or unhappiness in the future. Talking negative about your career with others at work — less likely for future promotion. Throwing golf clubs after bad shots — again pointless and a waste of money. Cussing like a sailor around others — not funny, cool or "in"... honestly, it's just not necessary. One thing to note is that many of these things are the "here-and-now / today" issues but over time, these situations change or go away all together.

Patience is an absolute critical success factor in personal relationships. Family relationships can at times be challenging and it takes a strong person to have patience in the face of difficult situations.

As I write this section, I think about the old saying "patience is a virtue" and I understand why. It is very difficult to manifest patience in our everyday lives due to the many outside influences affecting all aspects of our life (we will cover this later in the book). Things that are difficult are often the best to work on consistently as they impact other areas of our life. Is the patience song dancing around your head? If not, it will. Maybe there's a reason it is so catchy.

> *"Patience and perseverance have a magical effect before which difficulties disappear and obstacles vanish."*
> — John Quincy Adams

LOSE THE LANGUAGE!

"Mirror, Mirror, On my wall, Tell me who is the loneliest fool of all, No wait a minute, I believe I see, the answer staring back at me"
— Diamond Rio, *Mirror, Mirrror*

You are just oh so cool. I mean, doesn't everybody love a potty mouth? That must be what you are thinking as you drop the "f"-bombs left and right at work and at home. One person's opinion here, but I have to say that it almost makes me cringe when I hear someone going on and on using "trash mouth" language.

Unbelievably, some businesses accept this language as part of the culture. In fact, I just read an article in a popular technology magazine stating that cussing at work could actually help to create an environment of getting things done. That it is a way to ensure focus and press employees to go beyond. A mechanism by which an individual applies force to a situation. This culture would definitely not work for me and quite frankly, I find myself embarrassed for the individuals demonstrating this behavior on a regular basis. It's just not necessary.

I have not done my homework to better understand the origin of the most-favored cuss words. And, I won't waste my time.

Drop the language. It does nothing to benefit a business or personal situation. In most circumstances, it detracts. It tears someone down. It creates discomfort in a family environment. It demonstrates insecurity. It absolutely subtracts from the value of your personal brand. Interestingly enough, I frequently hear people refer to an individual because of his or her trashy language or negative behavior. How they treat and talk to people vs. the good things the individual may be doing. This one ties to the concept of self-monitoring and is important to consider.

INVEST IN PERSONAL RELATIONSHIPS

"And I don't see, How you could ever be, Anything but mine"
— Kenny Chesney, *Anything But Mine*

I will start by saying that I strongly debated even including a section on personal relationships in this book. I could write an entire book on that subject alone and I will — that's next on my list after my next album!

Personal familial relationships are a core component of your personal brand. Family and loved ones can be positive support when other areas of your life are maybe not going so well. These relationships can be a foundation on which you manage other weaker areas of your life. Your family and close personal friends are your support structure.

Relationships and family can also be a source of stress, pain, agony and angst bleeding over into your work performance, leadership activities, engagement with friends, and much more. Bottom line is that family relationships directly impact your personal brand.

Instead of trying to eloquently write a few paragraphs on dating, relationships, marriage, etc, I thought I would just outline a few key messages — take it or leave it (and watch for the "relationship" book in the future!).

- Don't be afraid of rejection. It will happen — move on
- Sometimes the right relationship is staring you straight in the face, and yet, somehow, you are not seeing it

- Trust and honesty are foundational elements of any and all relationships — without it, the relationship fails or is consistently in-flux
- Open and honest communication sounds easy and is actually difficult
- Text messaging and email are not good forms of "relationship communication"— pick up the phone and call or even better — discuss issues face-to-face
- Common core values are critical to lasting success together
- Be on the same page regarding family before you get married
- Having kids means re-prioritization and sacrifice — why have kids if you are not going to make time to teach them, be home for them, coach them, be available, or provide a good example for them?
- Find common ground in faith before exchanging wedding vows
- Money and finances are the root cause of many relationship beginnings — and endings
- Opposites attract but rarely last
- Everyone has issues; consider to what extent you are willing to accept the issues — are they deal-breakers?
- Never give up just because a few challenges develop in the relationship — talk about it, work it out, give it a chance
- Because your proverbial "clock is ticking" is no reason to settle

- Reserve the three words for the right person and mean it when you say it (no empty I love you's!)
- The grass is not always greener
- Cheat now, pay forever
- Divorce is not a get-out-of-jail-free card and should not be taken lightly
- Recognize that NOBODY knows your personal situation, your thoughts, ideas, opinions and feelings like you, especially after a divorce or relationship break-up — filter the opinions of others and do not allow those typically fact-less opinions to drive your life decisions
- And vice versa, keep in mind that you really don't know "what a person is going through" or "how they feel" or the emotions running through an individual in a difficult situation

COMPLETE THE PLAY

"It's Big time, Big plays, Prime time, Game day, It's Saturday in the South!"
      — Justin Honaman, *Saturday In The South*

Do you follow-through on commitments? At work? In your personal life? Do you drop the ball or shift work to others when you find that you have taken on too much? Do you hold yourself accountable? Are you checked-in?

Completing the play means that you follow-through on commitments. This concept applies to sports teams as much as to the office and home. When players on a college football team do not give 100% during a play or drive, the play often fails and could contribute to a big momentum swing in the game. All of this because one member of the team did not complete the play.

In the business world, commitments are made and when one fails to follow-through, trust and credibility with that individual or team are lost. Furthermore, work is delayed, business is lost, clients and / or customers are unhappy, and employees are adversely affected.

On the family front, completing the play means following-through on obligations made as far back as the day that you exchanged your vows. It means accepting responsibility for the kids in the evenings after your wife has had them all day. It means being at the kids' soccer games and dance recitals vs. drinks with the guys. It means being there for each other when difficult situations arise in the relationship. It means being fiscally responsible. It means being loyal to the commitment you made when you got married.

Complete the play!

Key Points

> ➢ **Make Time to Visit and Learn From Your Family**
>
> ➢ **Experience the World Together**
>
> ➢ **Have Patience**
>
> ➢ **Lose the Language!**
>
> ➢ **Invest in Personal Relationships**
>
> ➢ **Complete the Play**

CHAPTER 4

Work / Career: Work It Out!

Core Focus Area in Definition of Your Personal Brand

Life Lessons

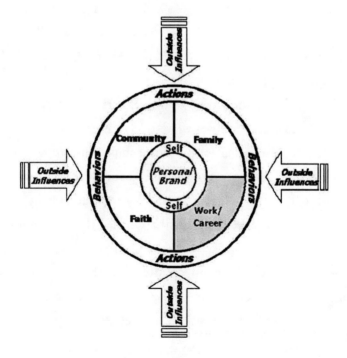

IT'S TRULY ALL ABOUT RELATIONSHIPS

"It's the real thing, nothin' can beat it, The pause that refreshes me, It's cool, hip-hot, rip-rockin', Catch the wave, get out, be free! Liquid Sunshine....Liquid Sunshine....Liquid Sunshine"
— Justin Honaman, *Liquid Sunshine*

Coca-Cola. What comes to mind when you read these words? Tradition. Advertising. Red. Mean Joe Green. Refreshing. Ice cold. A good mixer with Captain Morgan or Crown Royal! Liquid sunshine. Americana. The world. Big brand. Why is Coca-Cola one of the most recognized brands in the world?

Coca-Cola is a company that was built on strong relationships. It started as a fountain beverage at 5 cents a glass in 1886[3]. It sold primarily in pharmacies. In 1909, there were 400 bottling companies (74 remain today) serving North America. Today, Coca-Cola is a global brand.

Coca-Cola manifested an entrepreneurial spirit around the country as it's representatives aggressively invested their time and resources in developing local relationships with store owners, proprietors, maintenance workers, sports teams, stadium concession managers, high schools, colleges, and many, many others. It was these relationships that formed the foundation for growth that Coca-Cola experienced in its first 100+ years.

Success is truly founded on the strength of relationships. Companies that become too internally focused may quickly lose share, competitive position, market leadership, top talent

[3]For God, Country, and Coca-Cola: The Definitive History of the Great American Soft Drink and the Company That Makes It by Mark Pendergrast

and much more. Politics — meaning who's got what title, who reports to who, who has decision power and so on — begin to taint what is of utmost importance — a customer or business partner relationship.

At the end of the day, I may offer a great price and great product but in today's world, the competition is also offering great products and competitive prices. Who do I buy from? To whom do I allocate additional resources? What if I have a great relationship with the competitive sales representative? He lives in my town. She knows my business. He brings new ideas and presents them with dual benefit in mind.

Whether it is Coca-Cola or any other business — success is based on a team's ability to develop and maintain strong relationships with customers, partners and stakeholders. And deliver.

When I interview potential new-hires for a role, one of my personal criteria for consideration is whether I would feel comfortable placing this individual in front of an executive during a presentation. With a customer for a top-to-top meeting. Working with a partner on a collaborative project. At the end of the day, those with relationship management skills, not slick, "salesy" skills will consistently help the business achieve heightened success.

For seven years after college, I was in the consulting business starting at Ernst & Young, LLP. I worked on many different types of projects ranging from supply chain and lean manufacturing to activity-based management, CRM, strategic marketing and the list goes on. Each time we sold a project, our objective was to deliver on time, under budget, and exceed the client's expectations.

In addition, there was an "un-measurable" objective which was to build an outstanding relationship with the client so that there would exist the opportunity to position additional work or new projects. The primary criteria for decision-makers in moving forward with a new project or add-on work was the relationship with the consultants, with the consulting partner or with an account manager. I took time to get to know my client associates. I was interested not only in their background, experience, position and responsibilities at work, but also interested in their personal endeavors. I was not just on-site to bill time and expenses. I viewed myself as a personal advisor and someone in whom my client could trust.

Beautiful PowerPoint decks, flip charts, and Kinkos-bound brochures were impressive but it was the people that the client bought. It was the attitudes, behaviors, personalities, abilities, and values that the client bought.

If it's all about relationships, what are you doing to build them? To maintain them over time? To leverage them?

BE A PIONEER

"Don't give me no flack, I'm gonna push right back, I see the world with a glass half full, I don't need your negative energy friend, I'm staying focused, get r' done, Let's roll!"
— Justin Honaman, *Makin' It Happen*

> *"Just Git' 'r Done!"*
> — Jim Marvel *(my boss at Coke...via Larry the Cable Guy!)*

PI-O-NEER (*DICTIONARY DEFINITION*)⁴

1. One who ventures into unknown or unclaimed territory
2. One who opens up new areas of thought, research or development
3. Of, relating to, or characteristic of early settlers: the pioneer spirit
4. Leading the way; trailblazing

The pioneers. When I first joined Coca-Cola Customer Business Solutions, my boss Jim Marvel shook my hand, gave me a coon-skin cap and said, "Welcome to the team. We are pioneers!" I am quite sure the look on my face must have clearly depicted my reluctance but I thought the gesture nice. After all, we were starting a new organization. Hiring. Growing. Building. Charting new territory. Establishing an organization that spanned the entire Coca-Cola system: 70+ Coca-Cola bottlers, the Minute Maid Company, Foodservice, Odwalla, Glaceau to name just a few.

What I quickly recognized is that being a pioneer is much more than striking out into new territory. It is taking risks. It is challenging the way things have always been done. It is avoiding the political swirl that often encompasses large initiatives within major, hierarchical companies. It is stepping out and saying "no" while offering alternative options with the best interests of the business in mind. And, of course, the best interests of our people.

---

⁴ Google.com dictionary

It is putting in the extra effort to take a good result and make it great.

The reality is that organizations, like people, resist change. They seek stability, steady state and the comfort zone. As the book *The Leadership Challenge* clearly states, "Leaders must challenge the process precisely because any system will unconsciously conspire to maintain the status quo and prevent change." Progress requires change.

Perhaps one thing pioneers of the "old days" did best was to ply waters through new and unknown passages — to press on in the face of great fear, uncertainty and doubt.

One example of the "pioneering spirit" would be an experience I had several years ago with Lowes. I am a loyal Lowes shopper. Their stores are impeccable. Their customer service is top-notch. I enjoy the "experience" of shopping at Lowes. With my background in marketing, I could not help but wonder why they did not have some type of loyalty card or frequent shopper card program. Without it, how would they know "me?" How would they market and direct programs to "me", the consumer?

I decided to put together a presentation on consumer marketing opportunities I saw "at the shelf" and Fedex'd it to the Chief Marketing Officer at Lowes. Bold? Yes — but why not? Worst case, nobody responds. Maybe my ideas could help them improve the consumer experience.

About two weeks later, I received a call from the CMO's Executive Assistant requesting a conference call to discuss my presentation. I was blown away and honestly, impressed. We scheduled the call and he diligently reviewed each of my major points in detail. He shared with me Lowes' plans around each area and thanked me for sharing constructive ideas and opportunities vs. complaints and issues. At Lowes, the "little" tactical initiatives at the store level mean as much as the "big" strategic ideas.

I am also a loyal Delta Air Lines frequent flyer. I am more than happy to pay a higher fare to experience the consistent service offered by Delta and to enjoy the benefits of the SkyMiles program. For a number of years, I was a "Platinum Medallion" based on my flying more than 75,000 miles each year. Taking the same approach as I did with Lowes, I decided to offer observations and ideas for an improved customer loyalty program to Delta. I reached out to one of my business colleagues at Delta and she introduced me to the individual that runs the Delta SkyMiles program. To this day, I am very good friends with him and he welcomes new insights and ideas. He and I share ideas and challenge pervading thoughts together on a regular basis.

It is important to focus on opportunities, not problems. On solutions, not issues. On the "even-better-ifs" vs. the complaints. How often have you had an idea and not shared it? How many times have you had a great business concept and not pursued it? How often do you find yourself writing-off opportunities because of "no time" or "too much going on in life"? When was the last time that you offered insights on how to make a process, system, individual or organization better? How often are you the silent participant at a meeting, with a new idea or concern, often unshared or socialized? A leader is someone who has the courage to say publicly, what everyone else is saying privately — or not saying at all.

Step up when others choose the easy route. Raise your hand when others are not willing. Take on the small, "menial" tasks in the interest of learning, growing and contributing. Reach out to others with ideas and insights — challenge yourself to impact others. Make old pathways to success obsolete and choose the path less traveled.

I love Will Smith's perspective on hard work. He stated in a recent *60 Minutes* interview, "I've never viewed myself as particularly talented. I've viewed myself as ... slightly above average in talent. Where I excel is with a ridiculous, sickening work ethic. While the other guy's sleeping, I'm working. While the other guy's eating, I'm working. While the other guy's making love, I mean, I'm making love too, but I'm working really hard at it!"

Be a pioneer.

NETWORK WITHIN AND OUTSIDE OF YOUR FOUR WALLS

"That justice is the one thing you should always find, You got to saddle up your boys, You got to draw a hard line, When the gun smoke settles we'll sing a victory tune, We'll all meet back at the local saloon, We'll raise up our glasses against evil forces, Singing whiskey for my men, and beer for my horses"
　　　　— Toby Keith, *Beer For My Horses*

"It's the Network"
— Verizon Wireless

Harvard Business School is known for many things — at the top of the list, is the "network" one truly buys into upon completing their MBA. I have always been fascinated by the HBS connections. Around the world, HBS alums look out for one another. They offer unique opportunities to fellow alums. They stay connected. They trust in each other. Why? One never knows where there might be a need for guidance or assistance in the future from a "trusted" advisor. What an amazing network of business and philanthropic leaders.

Not everyone has the opportunity to attend Harvard Business School but there are many other mechanisms by which one may build a professional network.

When I think about networking, I separate the activity into three buckets:

- Inter-company network
    o With professionals inside your company of employment
- Intra-company network
    o With professionals working for other businesses outside of your own
- Community network
    o With associates from college, philanthropic and non-profit organizations

Do you take time to understand the structure, leadership, and culture of your business? Do you get involved in programs that touch many different aspects of your company? Do you attend the all-hands meetings? Have you invited someone from another part of the business to join you for lunch to share ideas and knowledge with your team? Have you read about the organization and taken time to appreciate its history? Do you make note of contacts discovered in other parts of the business?

It sounds simple but unless you make an effort, relationships and a professional network will not develop. Sitting in a cube, isolated from the world, will not strengthen your professional network. Nor will it contribute to long-term career success. Reach out and understand what other parts of the business are doing and invest in "inter-company" knowledge. Inter-company knowledge does not just include understanding org structures and hierarchy; it includes networking and relationships across the enterprise. Companies of all sizes offer structured opportunities to network with others in the company but it is up to each individual to determine how to best pursue the "un-structured" networking opportunities.

What about relationships across businesses or within an industry? There are many industry organizations that exist within most major cities catering to individuals with a common interest or background; thus strengthening intra-company networks. Some focus on technology, some on marketing, and others on arts and music. Yes, one must take the initiative to research and identify opportunities. The result could be an entirely new group of friends, colleagues or even a new career opportunity. These organizations are also excellent environments to better understand industry trends.

The third and final bucket is the community network. This network includes the friends and associates met through community philanthropic activities, civic boards, churches, college, and the list goes on. This is also an important group as it offers a mix of like-minded individuals and those with very different thoughts and ideas. I have personally found that the community network challenges my thinking in a way that I do not experience through the inter or intra-company networks.

There are a number of online tools enabling business relationships and interactions for each of the three networking buckets. One excellent example is Linked-In (www.linkedin. com). Linked-In is making waves online by enabling members to connect with current and past business colleagues, college classmates, and others with common interests. Through Linked-In, I have personally reconnected with many individuals that were on the "outer boundary" of my close circle of friends. I have also met many recruiters looking to place individuals and business associates with common career interests and goals.

A second example is Facebook (www.facebook.com). Facebook is a powerful "social" networking site with a different style and unique features that differentiate it from Linked-In, MySpace and other similar sites. For me, Facebook has allowed me to reconnect with many personal friends from high school, college and previous jobs. It is a true social networking site vs. business networking site.

The paper rolodex is obsolete. Today's rolodex is Microsoft Outlook, a Blackberry, an iPhone, online virtual networking sites and who knows what is just around the corner!

Either way, networking and your connections are a critical success component to the long-term viability of your personal brand. Invest in your network's growth, and increase the value of your personal brand. It's all about relationships. It's not "the" network, it's "your" network.

EXEMPLIFY OPEN AND HONEST COMMUNICATION

"All we need to do, Is make sure, We keep talking."
— Pink Floyd, *Keep Talking*

"When EF Hutton talks, people listen." Remember that old EF Hutton commercial? I am really not sure why, but I can remember tag-lines and jingles from old ads as if they were just on TV during the last commercial break for *24* or *Lost*!

I learn a great deal by watching others in leadership roles. I take note of communication styles. Verbal and non-verbal messages. Information shared with team members and peers. I learn from their hits and misses. When you speak to members of your organization or team, do they listen? Do they trust you? Do they take notes or do they interrupt and talk over you?

One lesson I learned from observation of a former boss was to be consistent in my communication. He espoused to many of us that he was an excellent leader. A very open, honest and transparent person with his team's every success in mind. He frequently would share "tidbits" of information with various members of his team. With no apparent rhyme or reason, he would share things that had not been shared or discussed with others on the team. He would also, on occasion, drop a "grand reveal" on the table as if to show that "I know this and you are the first to hear it … and you are hearing it first, from me!"

What he did not recognize was that the team, being a tight-knit group, would discuss regularly what had been told to them by the leader. They each had different pieces of information that the other had not heard. While exciting and interesting, this very quickly led to uncertainty, doubt, and distrust in the leadership.

Simple lesson: Communicate regularly. Do it tactfully (making a point without making an enemy). Demonstrate an interest in listening. Be honest. Be consistent. Ask for feedback.

Open and honest communication breeds trust, loyalty and devotion. Through the ups and downs of typical business cycles, employees are more likely to make the extra effort if they feel well-informed, engaged and involved. People do listen and at times when you least expect it. Communicate effectively and strengthen your personal brand value while positively impacting others.

LET SWITZERLAND BE SWITZERLAND!

"It's better to be hated for who you are, than be loved for who you're not"
— Van Zant, *Help Somebody*

> *"Switzerland: A magnificent country … but not a management style"*
> — Me!

For a number of years, I was a management consultant. I loved my work: the travel, the training, my clients, the variety of projects, new business relationships, interaction with top executives, the "professional" in professional services firm and the opportunity to work with global companies and understand worldwide cultures, perceptions, and priorities.

I also found that I worked very hard to make everyone happy. To be the guy that everyone liked. If there was a time when someone was upset or disappointed in me or my work, it was as if a major tragedy had struck my life. Like the air was punched right out of me. I worked hard to fix it. I attempted to please everyone. I apologized for anything that I could have possibly done wrong.

That's when reality set in. It's not possible to please everyone. I am not going to be everyone's "best" friend. I am not here to agree with everyone else. I have perspective, ideas, knowledge and skills of my own. They need to be represented — shared in a constructive way.

I first started catching on when a number of consulting managers started to call me "Switzerland". I thought it was funny at first but then realized that this was not me. I had quite a bit of business experience; relationships around the world, a rockin' resume of clients, projects, roles and responsibilities. People were interested in my ideas and insights and yet I was not serving them up. If those ideas potentially threatened to counter the ideas of another person, or cut against the political tide, or be one voice in the crowd, I would often withhold them or soften their meaning. I committed to change and found a happy medium between Switzerland and North Korea!

I now thrive on challenging the "system" way of thinking that exists within an organization — to offer alternatives that improve the overall organization and to offer direct advice and guidance.

I have learned to be an effective listener and to structure my comments, ideas and opinions in a way that is constructive and not destructive — I focus on the issues, not the person. I have learned to take a side, to have a fact-based platform and to make appropriate arguments. I am no longer Switzerland — I am now my own country.

Don't leave people wondering what you really meant to say. Follow through. Do what you say you are going to do. Don't be afraid to take a side, especially if you have facts to support an argument. You can not please everyone or be everyone's friend. You must be yourself — it's the only way to solidify your personal brand.

RECRUIT, COACH, MENTOR AND RETAIN THE BEST TALENT

"Guess who's the new talk of the town, The new S.O.B., The one everybody loves cuttin' down, Man it's a sight to see, They all smile right to his face, and hide their jealousy, Me I'm just working hard to get to that place, Where everybody hates me"
— Tim McGraw, *Everybody Hates Me*

> *"Get the right people on the bus ... and in the right seats"*
> — Jim Collins, *Good to Great*

As mentioned earlier in this book, one of my favorite books is *Good to Great* by Jim Collins. There are so many valuable concepts in the book and one that sticks out to me is to "get the right people on the bus."

Consider this. How many times have you looked around an organization, found many smart people, but still the operation is not a high-performance machine — a true team. Just because individuals are smart or nice does not make them the right fit for a team that is going to help the business take the necessary radical leaps to get to the next level.

In consulting, I worked with more than 30 multi-faceted businesses around the world. Each faced traditional and non-traditional business challenges. Each had its share of politics and people issues. And each struggled to get the right people on the bus and move the wrong people off of the bus. Typically, companies "pass-off" poor performers, or those that may not be the "best fit", to another part of the same organization. They struggle with the decision to let someone go. This is not fair to the individual or the business. The "it's not my problem any more" attitude is detrimental to the overall performance of the organization, to internal teams and to the individual. If it's not the right fit, move them on. It is in the best interest of everyone involved.

Additionally, companies often fail to put in place a recruiting and hiring system that identifies not only technical or business skills in prospective employees, but also their personality, people skills, potential to lead, and engagement in philanthropic or community activities outside of work.

Surround yourself with people of high potential. Never be afraid to hire others smarter, more flexible, or more knowledgeable than yourself. After reading numerous leadership books stating this exact principle, I still find that managers feel threatened and therefore, choose others that are "non-threatening" to fill roles on a team. Those that are weaker, not as smart, not the right people to move the organization forward. What a mistake.

Leaders surround themselves with individuals of even greater talent, skill and ability. A good leader is able to provide coaching and direction to talented individuals; allowing others to take credit for accomplishments and results.

As you recruit the right people for your organization, dedicate time to educating them. Who has helped you get to where you are today? Who has nudged you or provided you constructive performance feedback? How do you mentor others — do you recognize when others look to you and observe your actions as well as how you handle situations and people? Mentoring others is a way to give back and leave an imprint on the life or career of another person.

Encouragement is powerful in today's society. It could be a handwritten note card, an unexpected phone call or surprise visit to tell someone that you appreciate their work — that you recognize their efforts and have learned something from them. That you believe in them. Do not take this responsibility lightly. Treat associates like professionals; trust their judgment and coach mistakes.

***

I grew up watching Florida State football in Tallahassee, Florida. I loved Bobby Bowden and enjoyed watching him coach. I loved his perspective on the game of college football — and life. He once said that one of the greatest honors is to have coaches that he hires move up, and move on to even higher roles in the college and professional ranks. He attracts the best.

He works with the best. He mentors the kids on his team and his coaching staff. He is truly one of the best college football coaches in history. He was not afraid to hire others that could be smarter, faster, better than him. And look where he is today — still coaching winning teams and making a difference.

***

Finally, keep in mind that your top talent must be maintained aggressively. Often taken for granted or placed to the side in order to focus on poor performers, and with the assumption that they are self-sustaining, your top performers must consistently remain a focus for development and growth. Gerhard Gschwandtner[5] states that high achievers are:

- Driven by a pioneering spirit
- Impatient with those who seek safety and comfort
- Know that all horizons are artificial
- Focused on climbing higher, searching deeper, looking far back and at the same time looking far ahead

If you want to strengthen your personal brand then find the best talent, win their hearts and mentor them to mastery. Surround yourself with others that are stronger and smarter than you — and learn from them! A solid foundation comes from investing time and money in finding, cultivating and encouraging individuals with talent.

---

[5] Gerhard Gschwandtner, *Secrets of High Achievers*

ESTABLISH A PERSONAL BOARD OF ADVISORS

"I love this bar, It's my kind of place, Just walkin' through the front door, Puts a big smile on my face, It ain't too far, Come as you are, Mmmm, I love this bar"
— Toby Keith, *I Love This Bar*

Think back over your business and college career. Who strikes you as a true "leader"? Whose opinion do you value? Who has provided you with personal and / or professional coaching and guidance that has been spot-on? Who can you trust? Who really knows you? It is probably someone for whom, if they called today to discuss a career situation, professional need or personal challenge, you would absolutely make time.

When I was in consulting at Ernst & Young, I learned that one of our partners had established his own "personal" board of directors. He even organized regular meetings for the group to meet, share ideas, provide feedback on career decisions, and hold him accountable for commitments made.

I considered this concept as I developed my own personal and professional relationships working with different companies, miscellaneous volunteer organizations, and interfacing with leaders from all walks of life. I decided to leverage the concept and create my own "sounding" board if you will — individuals that I trust, will be honest and candid with their feedback, and will, most of all, enable me to better assess and make decisions.

I go to my board for feedback on any number of key life decisions. Do I convene them? No. I am able to solicit ideas and feedback via phone and email. Does the board constituency change? Absolutely! Over time, I "rotate" members on and off of the board based on their knowledge of my professional and personal situation. I simply keep their names on a list and leverage their insights and advice from time to time.

Make your list today! Who's on your board?

BE #1 AT CUSTOMER SERVICE

"Paper roses, Are making me blue, Paper roses, Remind me of you, Beautiful flowers that have no heart, Just like you, All they do is play a part,"
— Lola Dee, *Paper Roses*

Do you know Lola Dee? If you were in the military in Vietnam, you might know her from her performances with Bob Hope. You might also know her from her amazing recording performances including radio and television.

I met Lola in 1997 during my first visit to the Hyatt Regency Oak Brook, Illinois. Lola was and still is the concierge in the Hyatt's Regency Club (although the hotel chain name has since changed). Each night, I would leave my Ernst & Young project to return "home" to the Hyatt, eat dinner, exercise, and close out the night talking with Lola. It's another relationship that I find amazing. I am so thankful that we met and to this day, are still close friends. Another example of "it's funny how people are brought together"!

Anyway, Lola would go out of her way for guests of the Hyatt. She would schedule tours for visitors, she always took time to know the regular guests of the property, and she "connected" professionals from different companies who had similar backgrounds and interests. For many months, I had no idea that she was a singer (or used to be a singer) and it wasn't until an executive from McDonald's shared with me this fact, that I realized yet another of our connections. Lola was the reason that I spent each Monday-Thursday at the Hyatt.

Similarly, in Orlando, at yet another Hyatt (Hyatt Regency Grand Cypress), I was fortunate enough to meet Frank, Shirley, Mong and Sylvana during many visits to the property. I have not been to the Hyatt in over two years but if I walked in today, they would each know my name, my family, and know my history with the hotel. Oh, and not because they have a software system tracking this information. They took the time to get to know me during my previous visits.

One more example. I am passionate about "ultimate driving machines" (aka. BMW automobiles). What I appreciate most about BMW is that they have taken time to cultivate a relationship with me. To understand who I am. What I appreciate. BMW views me as a life-long customer. Not once has my BMW customer rep Tolli pressured me into a sale and she never will — that's just not her style. She is successful because of her relationship-building and "customer first" skills. Her approach yields dividends as her customers / friends refer their friends to her to buy vehicles. BMW is investing in long-term consumer relationships.

It's amazing what individuals can do for the success or failure of an organization or a brand. I could go on-and-on with numerous other examples of "being #1 at customer service" but

I think these three suffice. People buy from people they like — from people that care, from people that stand behind a product or service. What are you doing in your daily life with clients, customers, partners, family and friends to be "#1 at customer service"?!

ENCOURAGE AND PROMOTE ENTREPRENEURIAL THINKING

"...Shake ya tail-feather!"
— Nelly, P. Diddy, Murphy Lee, *Shake Ya' Tailfeather*

Entrepreneurs move and shake to their own beat. And the successful ones do "shake their tail-feathers"! Like no other group with whom I have ever been associated ... a unique breed. In my relatively short career, I have had the opportunity to witness and be a part of many different forms of entrepreneurship. While there are always exceptions, I have found a true lack of entrepreneurship in the larger, well-established corporations. The smaller firms allow for more freedom in decision-making, in ideation, in communication amongst all levels in the business.

Perhaps what has been the most discouraging is the lack of entrepreneurial, out-of-the-box thinking in larger companies. The ones that often have the largest bank account to fund new initiatives, innovation and new capabilities. What I found to be most common across enterprises was the desire by many to "squeak" by and not make a "dumb" or "wrong" decision (aka. Career Limiting Move

(CLM)) — to do just enough to get by then hand it off to the next person as they get promoted into a new role.

Furthermore, this was exaggerated greatly if that individual had a significant amount of company stock, options, pension program seniority, etc. The decision-making process in this environment is also a total cluster. Decision by committee, decision with 99% of the facts vs. 80-20, fear of failure, fear of "looking bad" or making a perceived poor decision and the list goes on.

These are the companies that are not able to move from "good to great" (quoting Jim Collins' book). These are the ones that are left behind by the competition. These are the ones drinking just a bit too much of their own Kool-Aid.

The entrepreneurial spirit starts with leaders and often at the top, but not always. As a leader, you have the opportunity to encourage this way of thinking daily: in your hiring, in your coaching, as you mentor others, as you establish culture policies, as you make difficult decisions, as you do what is right for the business and as you manage teams and provide structure or freedom for decision-making at all levels. This is the type of thinking that enables companies to take radical leaps — large gains, move an industry or market, make a difference and impact society.

Within the Coca-Cola System, I have had the opportunity to work with many incredible individuals. I "click" with individuals that are passionate about leadership, career development and doing what it takes to stay above the political swirl to get things done! These are the people that make tough decisions and lead change. That hire the absolute best talent to help our customers and move the company forward.

On a recent Delta flight from San Francisco to Atlanta, I spent two hours in the galley of the Boeing 757 discussing our organization and leadership with a business colleague, Cathy. I was particularly interested in her thoughts and ideas on entrepreneurial thinking. In her words, "First, I go out and find the absolute best talent for the organization and open position(s). Those individuals may or may not be within the company but they are the best that I can find and are excited to learn and grow. I empower and trust them to make decisions."

Cathy went on to say, "I would prefer to have members of our team make decisions efficiently and acknowledge that not all of them are going to be "the right" or "perfect" decisions. We all learn from positive as well as negative results from decisions. If I do not encourage, support and promote out-of-the-box thinking as well as decision-making ability, I place my team members in a box. And nobody operates well when placed in a very confined space — limited by politics, policies, egos and barriers. Over time, they explode, get frustrated and leave. And thus, we have done ourselves a dis-service, not to mention potentially impacted a customer relationship."

Not everyone has the entrepreneurial or creative mindset. Few are willing to take the kind of risk typically associated with a true entrepreneur. While this may be you, keep in mind that as a leader, you have the opportunity to surround yourself with others that bring this competency to the table. That can think outside of black-and-white. By encouraging this type of thinking, you not only strengthen the individual, you also strengthen the value of your personal brand. The best leaders surround themselves with others that are stronger and more knowledgeable.

DRINK THE KOOL-AID WITH CARE!

"Not since the day I left Milwaukee, Lynchburg, Bordeaux, France, had some of the best times, you never remember with me, Alcohol!"
— Brad Paisley, *Alcohol*

I admit that I love working for companies with a strong brand. I wear my company's logo lapel pin on my sport coat, always play the company golf balls, share excitement about new product launches with friends and family, and so on. It is not long before I am "drinking the proverbial company Kool-Aid" and feel "super-confident" in the products, services and experience offered by the organization.

Too much of the Kool-Aid, though, very quickly leads to arrogance, closed-mindedness, short-term thinking, personal career / life prioritization conflicts, lack of innovation, and a huge hangover! The same can be said for your personal brand. When a person gets too focused on "me", one often misses out on opportunities in life and fails to see what lies in front of them. They are passed over for promotion and quickly relegated to the outer sphere of relationships due to a nasty ego — ultimately missing out on personal relationships.

I once worked for an e-business strategy consulting firm in the late nineties. The stock market was going crazy. Venture capital money was chasing everything from TotalProduce.com to

ExtraDrawer.com and many others that have come and gone. When I joined the firm, we had three individuals within our supply chain strategy practice. Over 12 months, we quickly grew our team to more than 100 employees and business was booming. Our group was just one of several in the company and the stock price was skyrocketing at over $100 per share! The Kool-Aid was the best one could ever drink and was even mixed with a little Grey Goose! One could do no wrong.

Less than two years later, operating expenses were out of control, Accounts-Receivable was through the roof, and new opportunities dried-up like a lake-bed in the midst of a serious drought. The company was sold, the stock price was at less than $1 / share, huge valuations quickly shrunk to peanuts, and hundreds of consultants were forced to find new places of employment.

Be cautious in drinking the Kool-Aid … professionally and personally.

TAKE NOTES

"Life's a journey, not a destination!"
— Aerosmith, *Amazing*

Part of developing your personal brand is learning how to see trouble long before it arrives. To understand the proverbial "forest" and the "trees". To not miss out on a learning opportunity.

Authentic leaders establish themselves as people who have the foresight to take great notes at work — and other places where new concepts are learned. To learn through others and document key findings and life lessons. To be someone people go to for answers and ideas. Many talk the talk and few take the small step to take notes and review personal insights and perspectives.

I carry a notebook with me at all times. At work, I take detailed notes during meetings. In church, I write down sermon lessons and key concepts. Even when I don't have my notebook, I find myself taking notes. At speeches, presentations, working sessions — just about anywhere. I find myself "needing" to write down what I have learned. Most evenings of the week, I make notes on three key areas: 1) what I learned during the day, 2) people or experiences for which I am thankful, and 3) life lessons learned for the future.

This has served me well in my professional life as I am typically the "go-to" guy for meeting notes, follow-up, agendas and action items. So many people sit in meetings at work, do not write a thing on paper, and then proceed to ask questions after the meeting about a topic already addressed during the meeting. MAJOR pet peeve — and quite frankly, ignorant, rude and irresponsible.

I have found that many of my notes serve me well today just as they did ten years ago. I use the key points as material for many of my songs and actually have integrated many of the ideas into this book. It's a lot of fun to look back at meeting notes from my first few years in consulting, sermon notes from Dr. Stanley at First Baptist Church in Atlanta, and my "life lessons" notes that I have been writing many nights for a number of years.

Give it a try. Purchase a spiral-bound notebook today and see what develops. You might be surprised at the words that flow out of your Uni-Ball pen!

LIE NOW, PAY LATER

"Give 'em the old razzle dazzle, Razzle Dazzle 'em, Give 'em an act with lots of flash in it, And the reaction will be passionate, Give 'em the old hocus pocus, Bead and feather 'em, How can they see with sequins in their eyes?...Razzle dazzle 'em, And they'll never catch wise!"
— Chicago, *Razzle Dazzle*

It starts small. Over time it feeds on itself and becomes bigger and bigger until eventually, it is out of control. One small lie. One "meaningless" secret. Lies are like secrets — they are just about impossible to keep from others.

In business, managing expenses is critical to ensuring long-term viability of any business. I will never forget an experience I had with one of my former employers. One of our VP's felt that the company "owed" him for the many extra hours he had to work. Soon, expense reports grew and the stack of cab receipts was being taped to sheets of paper to "compensate" him for the "inconvenience" of having to work the extra time. What's amazing is that he felt assured, comfortable, justified, in taking this action. He had talked himself into this activity being acceptable. He was eventually let go by the company for a number of reasons, one of which was expense management, another for secrets that he was harboring outside of the office. It really does catch up with you over time. Don't flush your career over small change.

Lying frequently goes beyond business relationships and often extends into personal relationships. Have you heard the word "smarmy"? Here is the official definition:

SM-AR-MY (DICTIONARY DEFINITION)[6]

1. insincerely, self-servingly, or smugly agreeable or earnest;
2. unpleasantly and excessively suave or ingratiating in manner or speech

If you travel regularly, you have probably seen "that group of men" — wrinkled Duckhead shorts, braided belt, Cole Haan shoes, no socks, Brooks Brothers polo shirt with logo, slicked-back hair, and staring down every half-way decent looking woman that walks past imagining "what if". Away from the wife, the kids and the wedding ring safely left upstairs in the hotel room. Being a "man" with "the guys"! Ahhh yeah!

Think about the personal brand image burned into the memory of your colleagues and the potential impact to your personal relationships. Decisions made out of town, away from home, in secret, do have significant consequences. Decisions made in the workplace and in personal relationships have consequences. As my good friend, and Buckhead Church leader, Jeff Henderson once stated, "We are never as alone, as when we are left alone with our secrets."

Take action to change your behavior. I would ask your conscience to play a major role in defining what is right and

---

[6] Google.com dictionary

wrong and trust its message. Lie now, pay later. Believe it. Deal with it. Or settle for the ramifications over time.

ALWAYS HAVE A BACK-UP PLAN

"Let's go...If you want it you can get it, Let's Go"
— Trick Daddy, *Let's Go*

Four months ago, I had breakfast with one of my best friends David. He shared with me that a number of partners at his law firm had decided they were going to break away from the parent firm and they were going to start their own practice. They invited David to join them as they recognized his excellent work, professionalism and relationship management skill set.

David shared with me some of his concerns regarding the potential move including family concerns — his wife was not working and was home with their two kids (one of which was a year old). This, in addition to questions regarding whether existing customers would follow them to a new firm, weighed on his mind.

I asked him one simple question. What is your back-up plan? What would you do if it does not work out? In fact, what would you do TODAY, if you were told that you were out of a job? Who would you call? Is your resume up-to-date? Do you have finances in order — just in case? Have you prayed about it? If you have a solid back-up plan, your options are greater and you can at least consider the new opportunity.

If you had to make a career move tomorrow, what would be your first steps? Who would you call? What actions would you take? Where would you go? What is the status of your business network? Your personal brand is a big player in decisions that can at times be difficult. A strong personal brand allows a person to more clearly make life-changing decisions. The world is not perfect and we all know the saying about best-laid plans.

WRITE THANK-YOU NOTES

"You better know that in the end, It's better to say too much, Than to never say what you need to say again, Say what you need to say, Say what you need to say"
— John Mayer, *Say*

Every Monday morning I write at least 4-5 notes on personalized stationary to thank or recognize individuals. It is part of my weekly routine. It makes a difference and is truly appreciated by the receiver.

Growing up, I wrote letters and notes all of the time to friends and family far and near. Email did not exist and phone calls were expensive. As society has moved into the digital age, communication via email, instant message and text message have taken the place of written communication.

From a "senders" perspective, I enjoy taking a few minutes to think about what I appreciate about the individual. What they have done well. How they have made an impact. Their importance in my life. Their value to our organization. It is time well spent as it establishes a weekly routine of appreciating others. I write these notes to members of my team at work as well as others I interact with outside of work to thank them for their outstanding efforts or even offer a bit of advice or encouragement.

From a "receivers" perspective, it is something that was not hastily thrown together. Something that required thought and time. And is something that can be kept for future reference.

It is an inexpensive and yet powerful way of thanking others. Recognizing amazing performances. Providing an uplifting thought at just the right time. Putting oneself out there in an authentic way for someone else.

Try it.

Key Points

> ➤ It's Truly All About Relationships
>
> ➤ Be a Pioneer
>
> ➤ Network Within and Outside of Your Four Walls
>
> ➤ Exemplify Open and Honest Communication
>
> ➤ Let Switzerland be Switzerland!
>
> ➤ Recruit, Coach, Mentor and Retain the Best Talent
>
> ➤ Establish a Personal Board of Advisors
>
> ➤ Be #1 at Customer Service
>
> ➤ Encourage and Promote Entrepreneurial Thinking
>
> ➤ Drink the Kool-Aid With Care!
>
> ➤ Take Notes
>
> ➤ Lie Now, Pay Later
>
> ➤ Always Have a Back-up Plan
>
> ➤ Write Thank-You Notes

CHAPTER 5

Faith: The Faith Factor!

Core Focus Area in Definition of Your Personal Brand

Life Lessons

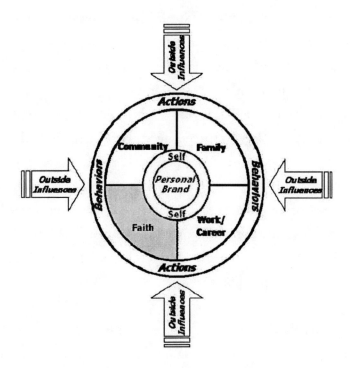

INVEST TIME IN YOUR FAITH

"Glorious one, Glorious one, Light of the world, You outshine the sun, King of all kings, Eternity sings, Glorious one,"
— Steve Fee, *Glorious One*

How do you define faith? What role does faith have in your everyday life? At work with your team? In relationships? At home with the family? How does faith fit into your personal brand model? Are you hesitant to read this chapter of the book? For me, faith is the most important aspect of my personal brand. While it is depicted as a "quadrant" on my brand model, it is truly intertwined in each of the other areas of the model.

Andy Stanley, pastor of North Point Community Church in Alpharetta, Georgia stated in a recent message, "There is a hole in your heart that neither people nor things can fill ... only God and your relationship with Him can fill it."

I always find it interesting to meet new people, especially in places that I least suspect. I recently traveled to Anchorage, Alaska to visit a Coca-Cola bottler. I stayed at the Sheraton and was visiting with the concierge one afternoon — she was originally from India. I asked her about her life. How she arrived in Anchorage. It was a very quiet afternoon and she opened up to me (for some reason this seems to happen to me regularly – which I enjoy and appreciate):

"I spent seven years with a guy. He told me he had all the money he ever needs and does not need to work — we moved to Anchorage. He decided after we moved that he did not want to get married and

so we broke up. I had a nervous breakdown. The whole world was dark. I did not know where to turn. My friends told me to go to dance clubs to meet guys, dirty dance, have sex that I won't remember, etc. But all I could do was go home and pray in my bedroom. My whole world was dark.

I saw a church across the street from my apartment and decided to stop in to ask if they had open times for silent prayer. They gave me the daily times and I went. I was crying profusely from my heart. I prayed with my whole heart. In the night, my friends came — I love my friends, but they wanted to go out partying and yet, I just enjoyed finding time to open the Holy Bible and read.

As I read, I discovered so many things that are truly applicable to my life. It was like reading a novel — so helpful at that moment of crisis. I realized that my parents were such great advisors when things were lost. Their faith was amazing and I miss them as they are both no longer living.

I found answers, hope and comfort in my readings and in my new friends at church. It is so important to me. You know, I had a big house, incredible trips, many friends, and yet, something was still missing. I was happy but then it was so quiet — the emptiness was there. I now go to church and someone says, "Welcome!"... I feel fulfilled. I have found purpose and direction in my life through the church and what I read in the Bible."

For those without a strong faith, I would encourage you to ask questions. Be open to new ideas. Ask yourself what you believe. Make the investment of time. Learn how to be humble and manage highs and lows. We are walking in this life but we must find time to develop a relationship with God.

An acquaintance once told me that he had a hard time with faith. "I don't see miracles every day," he stated. "I really struggle to understand why bad things happen. Why did 32 people die at Virginia Tech? If there was a God, wouldn't he prevent this from happening? It's not that I don't believe, I'm just not sure I believe. I guess I am agnostic — not atheist." I left a lunch with him knowing that the reasons to believe are all around us; that the unexplainable is only understandable via a strong, secure faith. Maybe it's because I understand my beliefs. My relationship with God. Maybe it's just taking a step back to appreciate some of the very simple things that exist in our lives today. Starting with our existence.

What would you say if someone shared these stories with you? How would you respond? It's truly interesting to me to meet someone that is looking, searching, hoping that someone will give them a reason to believe. Someone will provide answers. A direction. An example of a "miracle."

Recently, my close friend Jan Smith[7] (of Jan Smith Studios) was interviewed for an article in the Atlanta Journal-Constitution. She closed the interview with a striking comment that I could not help but to read over and over. When discussing her career, and potential next steps, she stated, "I don't know what the next

---

[7] www.jansmith.com

piece will be, but if I died today, there is nothing I hunger for more than to go out doing God's will."

I will close this segment with a few questions. Where do you think you will go when you die? What will be your legacy? What impact will you have made on others? On your community? On the world? On an individual? How will friends and family remember you? What will you be most thankful for ... and potentially regret?

God has a plan for your life. It just might not be presented to you in your desired way, shape or form. Or in your timeframe.

RECOGNIZE THAT LIFE DECISIONS DETERMINE YOUR ULTIMATE DESTINATION

"I will be strong, Even if it all goes wrong ... When I'm standing in the dark, I'll still believe, Someone's watching over me ..."
— Hilary Duff, *Someone Is Watching Over Me*

I love this quote from John Maxwell[8]; "We make decisions at different stages in our life and manage those decisions the remainder of our lives." The decisions you make throughout your life truly determine your destination. Which paths do you choose to take? Why? What drives your decision-making process? How do you make relationship decisions? Career decisions? What actions do you choose in ethical dilemmas? How do you treat others?

I first took note of this concept at a John Maxwell Maximum Impact session in 2005. I took down the idea, integrated it into

[8] www.maximumimpact.com

my regular thought process and then, two years later, as I was listening to a sermon series entitled *Destinations* by Andy Stanley, the concept arose again.

It absolutely makes sense. Decisions we make in college, we live with after college. Decisions we make in our 20's, we live with in our 30's. Good intentions do not get you to a necessarily positive destination. Ignore this fact, and you will wake up with poor options.

Why do so many individuals allow themselves to settle and not take a step forward — not find the right relationship, not make the best career move, not find the time to appreciate the many gifts in life, not make things happen?

"The direction or path you choose, determines your destination. Hopes, dreams and good intentions do not determine the destination," states Andy. "Take action, sacrifice and be willing to sustain some embarrassment then experience the relief from taking action — taking a path in the right direction toward a faith-filled destination." Be willing to endure the personal, political and familial consequences, and move on.

As much as we often make quick decisions based on experience, recognize that there are implications to decisions made for the wrong reasons or based on foundational principles made of sand — easily washed away by the tide.

Andy made it even clearer in stating the following in a way that I had not considered:

> "*Pride* overrides *Wisdom*,
> *Arrogance* overrides *Common Sense*,
> *Self-Importance* overrides *Discernment*"

SAMPLE AND FIND YOUR FAITH HOME

"You are the everlasting God, The everlasting God ... You do not faint ... You're the defender of the weak ... You comfort those in need ... You lift us up on wings like eagles!"
— Lincoln Brewster, *Everlasting God*

What is your favorite flavor of ice cream? Easy question and nothing to do with faith, right? Wrong! My favorite ice cream flavor is Cookie Dough with Cookies n' Cream coming in a close second.

Honestly, churches are a bit like ice cream. They each offer a different religious "flavor" to sample. Some are large. Some are small. Some are very formal. Others are laid-back and casual. There are churches at the beach and churches in the hills. Some with steeples. Some with neon signs. Churches are everything from "fire, hell, and-brimstone" to "mom, dad and apple-pie".

One thing is for sure. There is not one church for everybody. My experience with churches here in Atlanta has been very interesting. I have lived in Atlanta since arriving in 1991 to attend Georgia Tech. I have learned more about my faith and beliefs in the last ten years, than I ever did growing up going to church regularly in Florida.

My faith journey over the last ten years is an interesting one. I started going to an Episcopal church in downtown Atlanta while in college. I grew up always attending an Episcopal Church and this seemed like a logical choice. It was similar to what I was used to growing up but I really did not get much out of the services, sermons or Sunday school. Quite frankly, I felt like I was wasting my time on Sunday mornings and learning nothing.

I then made one of the greatest discoveries of my life. I visited First Baptist Church of Atlanta based on the suggestion of several fraternity brothers who attended regularly. Dr. Charles Stanley was preaching and his son, Andy Stanley, was in a leadership role at the church under his father. I was blown away; not only by the message, but the music, and the passion for learning so evident in its members.

For the first time ever in my life, I took notes at church. I bought my own bible. I started a notebook of my key learnings and observations, as well as notes on how to apply the key sermon points to my daily walk with life. (To this day, I still review and learn from my sermon notes from college.)

Andy left First Baptist in the mid-1990's to establish a new church, which became North Point Community Church in Alpharetta, Georgia. A number of my fraternity brothers and best friends from college started going there, attending programs during the week, assuming leadership roles within this new ministry, etc. and I started to learn more about this new church community.

What is truly amazing is that Dr. Charles Stanley now preaches to several thousand people every Sunday at his church in Chamblee, Georgia and speaks through the *In-Touch Ministry* to hundreds of thousands if not millions around the world. His son Andy now has a ministry spanning more than three major church campuses in the Atlanta area, several affiliate churches and impacts thousands of individuals each week. And oh, by the way, this ministry developed in less than 10 years!

These ministries are amazing in that they truly reach so many individuals and impact lives around the world. But wait … their teaching styles could not be more different.

Lectures, notes, suit, tie, big-band, "Baptist" choir, Sunday School and *Victory in Jesus* vs. Tommy Bahama, khakis, jeans, Starbucks coffee, Diet Coke, bright lights, flat screen TV's, smoke, Christian rock, small groups and even sermons on HD-video most Sundays. They cater to completely different audiences. And yet, they each base their teachings on the same foundation — the Bible.

I learn a great deal not only on Sundays, but also through other programs and activities that run throughout the week — including a *Life Lessons Over Lunch* series that is offered at my workplace. I learn concepts that I can apply to my everyday life.

I pay attention to the message each Sunday. I meet new people regularly. I am excited to help others develop a relationship with God. I am thrilled to have the opportunity to serve as a volunteer and leader on a regular basis. I love the service music and I have a total blast using my singing talents with kids programs. I see the church's impact on individuals, couples and families. And most importantly, their children who have yet to make their own decision on faith. It is "seeker-friendly" and I love it. It reminds me so much of my experiences at Blue Ridge (see earlier references) and ties back to the time when I accepted God in my life.

There are many churches in this world. Many of them do not truly teach the message of God. Many sermons include stories, jokes and games and are not centered on the scripture and how to apply it to your life. Many *tell* you to "obey" something without your first understanding, asking questions, interpreting, and making up your own mind. Many will criticize other faith communities that are growing and thriving. Sadly, most are only an illusion of what God intended church and a faith-friendly learning environment to be (as referenced by my church leader Jeff Henderson in one of his absolute best sermon series entitled *Illusions*).

Do you find yourself making your grocery list, picking out a lunch spot, thinking about shopping, sending text messages or whispering non-stop during a church service? Are you going beyond checking the proverbial church box each Sunday?

There are many flavors of ice cream out there; some taste better than others. Some you would never buy again and some, you would buy again and again every week because it is fulfilling. If you are not finding the spiritual truth in your church, take time to visit, explore and take a step outside of your comfort zone. Step into a new church. Try a new Sunday school class. Join a small group. Raise your hand to get involved. Find a faith home. A community where you may live and grow.

I love movies! In *Indiana Jones and the Last Crusade*, Harrison Ford is pursuing the "cup of Christ" and in the process, he must complete several challenges in the final pursuit. During one scene, he takes a blind step out over a chasm with faith that somehow he will not fall. Sure enough, there is a bridge on which he lands. He took a step based on faith and found a firm foundation on which to complete his journey. Not much different than our everyday lives.

Take action. Move beyond attending church on Christmas and Easter or attending for the wrong reasons. Faith is a key personal brand focus area — without it, structures crumble.

DEFINE YOUR SPIRITUAL GIFTS ... AND RECOGNIZE THEM IN OTHERS

"You saved my heart, From being broken apart, You gave your love away, and I'm thankful everyday, For the gift,"
— Collin Raye, *The Gift*

One of my favorite Christian concepts is that of spiritual gifts. Spiritual gifts are given to each of us so that we may teach others, serve friends and family, lead teams, set a positive example, and much more. On the surface, at times, they may be difficult to recognize. But with some study, they are more evident. Examples of spiritual gifts include Prophecy, Mercy, Teaching, Exultation, Giving, Leadership and Service and are best defined in Romans 12:6-8.

*"We have different gifts, according to the grace given us.
If a man's gift is prophesying, let him use it in proportion to his
faith. If it is serving, let him serve;
if it is teaching, let him teach;
if it is encouraging, let him encourage;
if it is contributing to the needs of others, let him give generously;
if it is leadership, let him govern diligently;
if it is showing mercy, let him do so cheerfully.*
— Romans 12:6-8

While my intention is not to write a Bible study or Sunday sermon, I have found that understanding your own spiritual gifts is critical to better understanding your situational behaviors as well as the behaviors of others. This, in turn, contributes to your personal brand.

Two very good friends of mine, Susan and Jennifer, stick out in my mind as individuals with a very unique gift — something they did not learn in college or from their work in a specific industry. They understand people. They can read a situation quickly and perceive the positive and potential negative outcomes. They are both very successful — especially in the areas of relationship management, change leadership, and organizational effectiveness. They both have the gift of Prophecy — I recognize it and we have discussed it. It is so incredibly interesting and at times, unbelievable. They recognize things that most people miss.

I took time to learn about spiritual gifts and also determined where they were best represented in my life and how I was using them. What impact I was making because of them. How I was being perceived by others through my actions and beliefs. Similar to a personality profile or test, we each have specific spiritual gifts.

For me, I have found that my primary spiritual gift is in the area of Leadership or Administration. I understand the characteristics and how my actions could be misunderstood by others. Honestly, when I put together my notes from different interpretations of this gift, I was blown away at how accurate it really was to my daily life. Let me outline my interpretation of the definitions for the other spiritual gifts. Note that these are my notes from different speakers (including Dr. Charles Stanley and Andy Stanley) and are not directly from one defined source.

PROPHECY

- Strong need to express self verbally
- Strong sense of right and wrong
- Do not hesitate to speak up
- First to see "evil" and speak out about it
- Ability to discern character and motives
- React harshly to deception and dishonesty
- Always looking at future
- Committed and jump in wholeheartedly
- Very open about own faults
- Loyal to truth vs. people
- Persuasive in defining truth
- Eager to make things plain and simple
- Wants to get to the bottom line
- Public boldness and strict standards could hinder intimate personal relationships

SERVICE

- Sees and meets practical needs
- Can not sit back and watch a need go unmet
- Disregard weariness and keep pressing on
- Difficult to say no
- Very alert to likes and dislikes

- Amazing ability to remember friends, places, and other details about people
- Giving continually to others
- Strong desire to be with other people as this leads to new opportunities to serve
- Need for approval and appreciation
- Always just a step ahead
- Desires to meet needs quickly – no "red tape" or committees
- Takes great delight in getting job done
- Focuses on achieving goals
- Tendency to feel inadequate
- Could appear pushy
- Disregard of personal need could extend to one's family

LEADERSHIP / ADMINISTRATION

- Ability to see the big picture and visualize the final result
- Ability to break down the big picture into smaller pieces and achievable tasks and think ahead
- Motivated to be organized in a given area of responsibility
- Strong desire to succeed and lead
- Insight to identify who can get the work done
- Tendency to remove self from distracting details and focus on the ultimate goal
- Willingness to endure negative reactions or rejection
- Perceived by others at times of being insensitive

- Require loyalty and confidence from those who are being directed and served
- Tendency to assume responsibility if no structured leadership exists
- Desire to complete tasks quickly and move on to the next steps
- Joy and fulfillment in seeing all parts come together and others receiving credit
- Strong sense of humility

MERCY

- Ability to feel atmosphere of joy or distress in an individual or group
- Attracted to and understand people who are having mental or emotional distress
- Desire to remove hurts and bring healing to others
- Sensitive to words and actions that may hurt others
- Cheerful and joyful
- Ability to sense genuine love
- Greater vulnerability to deeper and more frequent hurts from lack of love
- Vulnerable and often hurt in relationships
- Wired for loyalty and devotion
- Need to measure acceptance by physical closeness and quality time together
- Avoids firmness
- At times is hard to get to know

TEACHING

- Strong desire to present truth systematically
- Lay things out in orderly fashion
- Requires thoroughness
- Writes in consecutive order
- Desires to be detailed and thorough
- Needs to validate information that is received
- Ask lots of questions – enjoy the details
- Wants to check out others – credentials, background, etc.
- Great delight in studying and researching
- May appear prideful of their learnings
- May appear to be critical when one finds errors in facts

EXULTATION / EXHORTATION

- Purpose is to encourage
- Willing to share own weaknesses
- Desires to turn problems into opportunities
- Welcomes "lessons learned"
- Perspective is better to have pain today and pleasure tomorrow
- Want to know that they have been heard
- Desire to gain insights through personal experience
- Seeks harmony between diverse groups
- Appear to over-simplify problems
- May appear to disregard feelings of others
- Naturally wants to see results

GIVING

- Not solely about wealth / money
- Ability to understand available resources and choose where to invest / spend
- Expand resources wisely and plan ahead
- Careful with money
- Desire to give high-quality things
- Greatest satisfaction is giving of time and resources to the benefit of others
- Delight in giving without receiving credit
- Buy things of lasting value
- Often gives to motivate others to give
- May appear to want "control" of decisions / situations
- Frugality appears to friends and relatives as selfish

Try it for yourself. Do the research. Take time to learn about your spiritual gifts today – and define yours. Enjoy the experience!

IT IS WHAT IT IS … !

"If you want to hear God laugh, tell Him your plan,"
— Van Zant, *Help Somebody*

Perhaps one of the most popular, or should I say over-used, sayings that I have heard in the last two years — "It is what it is." I even find myself over-using it. It reminds me of when everyone was using "Tipping Point" in every other sentence.

While it annoys me to hear the saying so frequently, I actually appreciate the message especially when it comes to faith. God has a plan for our lives. It is not necessarily, and most likely is not, what you believe is the plan for your life. Many of us spend time worrying daily about things we just can't control. We concern ourselves with matters that in a day, week, month or year, really won't matter.

It is what it is. If your plan is not working, it could be a good time to ask for guidance from someone that owns your life's navigation system. It is completely natural to think that we can make all of the "right" decisions, connect with the right people, choose the best paths to follow — the ones that make us happy — and yet still, just when things seem to be falling right into place, out of nowhere comes an unexpected surprise and we are back at square one.

God's plan is what it is — His plan. Not ours. Take time to listen. To reflect. To pray and ask for guidance.

Key Points

> **Invest Time in Your Faith**

> **Recognize That Life Decisions Determine Your Ultimate Destination**

> **Sample and Find Your Faith Home**

> **Define Your Spiritual Gifts ... and Recognize Them in Others**

> **It Is What It Is ... !**

CHAPTER 6

Community: Giving Back

Core Focus Area in Definition of Your Personal Brand

Life Lessons

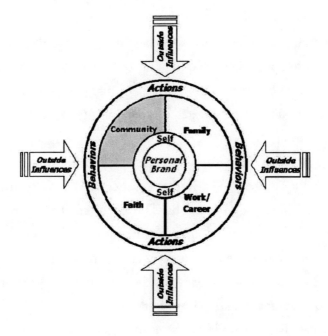

MAKE MAGIC HAPPEN

"Everyone's got a laughin' place, A laughin' place, To go, go, go, Take a frown, Turn it upside down, And you'll find yours we know!"
— Disney, *Laughin' Place*

For most people, this one is way down the list. I mean, on top of the dinner dates with your wife, swim meets for the kids, dinner at mom and dad's, long hours and out-of-town meetings for work, happy hours with friends, and more, how can there be any time to actually commit to a community activity?

One simple message: We all have the opportunity to make a difference in the lives of others — will you take advantage of those opportunities?

We all have the ability to bring "magic" into the lives of others through giving, volunteering our time, or serving as a volunteer. This can be accomplished in many ways and one of those is through time dedicated to a community or philanthropic organization.

Do you have a passion for kids organizations? Museums? Community centers? The Boy or Girl Scouts? Church outreach programs? Boys and Girls Clubs? The Y? You might be surprised at how small things go a long way in the world of "giving back". Every dollar and every hour truly does count. Often overlooked, this focus area is one that can positively impact *your own* life in addition to impacting the lives of others.

It can be as simple as planting trees, volunteering at a humane society shelter, sorting food at a community food bank, delivering meals to the elderly and sick that are not able to leave their homes, or visiting a nursing home to sing songs, play the piano or join in a card game for a few hours over a fried chicken lunch. This is also one of those areas where it is great to include a significant other, family members or friends.

Only a few months ago, I had the opportunity to sing our national anthem for a group of more than 2,400 Boy Scout leaders from across the country. During the program, I sat next to Steve Fossett who at the time was Chairman of the National Eagle Scout Association (of which I am a member). What amazed me about spending just an hour with him and his wife over breakfast was his true interest in giving back. In making a difference in the lives of others. That he had a passion for leading and for teaching leadership fundamentals to boys active in scouting. Steve was a successful businessman. Entrepreneur. Adventurist. I was so excited to hear his thoughts on making things happen. Just a few weeks later, Steve disappeared on a flight over the Nevada desert. The picture on my desk of Steve, my dad and I takes on new meaning. The one hour we had together meant a great deal to me and I look forward to passing on those thoughts and ideas to others interested in learning and growing through the Boy Scout program. Steve would be what I would term an incredible "Outside Influence" that truly impacted my life in a positive way.

As I write this book, Steve and his plane have not been found. I pray for him and his family. God has an interesting way of intersecting individual lives. When you least expect it. In ways that only He comprehends.

Do you recognize the impact you make on others in the small and large ways? You too can make magic happen in the lives of others.

PAY IT FORWARD

"I play guitar and I sing my songs in the sunshine, Captain and Cokes and barroom jokes keep me feeling fine, And there's always a stage and a beautiful babe to squeeze my lime, In my simple way I guess you could say that I'm living in the Big Time!"

— Big and Rich, *Big Time*

One of my favorite books, movies and concepts *pay it forward*. This concept was even replicated in a recent Liberty Mutual television commercial that I absolutely loved for its message beyond the advertising. Most, would probably not remember that it was an ad for Liberty Mutual, but do remember a person helping another helping another and so on throughout the commercial until finally, it comes full circle back to the first person.

The concept is simple — you do something for another person, they do something for another because of the perceived "feel-good" benefit of the experience, and so on. What's important to recognize is that *paying it forward* is something to live by. Not a one-time event or a check box or a one-and-done activity. What you give to others, will come back to you times ten. This idea has always intrigued me. I do believe that everything comes back around full circle — for better or worse. Treat someone poorly or with a mean spirit, and at some point, it will catch up with you.

Do good things. Help others. Financially support a charity or church without expectation of naming rights, a plaque or some other worldly recognition. Expect good things.

It's just so simple. And yet, so many people in today's society are completely focused on themselves and what is important to them — what will make them look good. Or feel important. Or boost an already over-sized ego. The reward that comes from giving time, money or in any other way, is much more fulfilling than a silly trophy or shiny coin.

The concept also reminds me of a phrase we used regularly when I was a Boy Scout: *Do a Good Turn Daily*! This is the Boy Scout slogan and it was impressed upon me weekly as a young man in Boy Scout troop 109 in Tallahassee, Florida. My experience in Boy Scouts was one that I did not truly appreciate until after my time was complete in the Scout troop. I had many incredible experiences as a Boy Scout: hiking the Appalachian Trail, spending a hot summer week at Boy Scout camp, exploring amazing beaches and parks, rafting down the white water of Tennessee's Chattooga River, canoeing the spring-fed rivers in North Florida, learning to tie knots and start a fire without matches, waking up in a warm sleeping bag with a frozen nose.

Of all things, my Boy Scout experience, to this day, provides me a framework by which to live my life — a motto to live by. It's a slogan by which our world would be a better place if even a few more followed. I am so very proud to be an Eagle Scout and honestly, I completed the Eagle Scout requirements thanks to my dad's support and encouragement. So many friends and colleagues share with me that they "wish" they had followed through and completed the path to Eagle Scout.

Scouting teaches foundational "Self" components in boys during influential youth years. Boy Scouting teaches teamwork, leadership, and so many other foundational traits that no other program could ever hope to instill in a classroom environment. There is not one day that goes by that I do not think about the "Good Deeds" I did or did not do in a given day.

It is interesting and not surprising that so many Eagle Scouts are in executive leadership roles throughout many organizations in our country today (Note: Read about some of these leaders in Alvin Townley's book *Legacy of Honor*).

So pay it forward. What good deed have you done today for someone else?

> *"You have been faithful in a small matter so I will put you in charge of ten cities."*
> — Luke 19:17

TOAST FOR CHANGE!

"I'm doin' the drop n' swap, Three dates n' then I walk, Turn it on n' turn it off, I'm doin' the drop n' swap"
> — Justin Honaman, *Drop n' Swap*

Three DVD envelopes arrived in my mailbox from *Netflix* last week. One of the movies was one that I had heard little about but found interesting in reading the movie summary and reviews. Surprisingly, *Freedom Writers* turned out to be my inspiration for this small section of the book.

"A toast for change" is an axiom used by the students in *Freedom Writers*. What an absolutely perfect concept. I traveled to Amsterdam in February and visited the Anne Frank house. I knew of her story but was not fully in-the-loop regarding her writings. What I found most interesting in the message of both the movie and the story of Anne Frank was the passion and focus on one person's ability to impact so many others — both directly and indirectly. Maybe not immediately, but over time.

It really doesn't matter what others say, as long as we believe in ourselves, are true to ourselves and follow our heart, we can all make a difference. Maybe in the life of one other individual. Maybe in the life of an entire organization. Or individual teams. A city, country or even globally.

And yet, it all starts with a penchant or openness to change. A willingness to take a difficult step. To stand up for what is right and good in this world. To help others that do not have the best "example" to look up to. To reach out and pick up others needing a helping hand. To be excited about possibilities and not focused on security or comfort. To not settle for the easy way out.

CONSIDER YOUR LEGACY

"Let me be a shining light for you, Let me be a joy to you always,"
— Kevin Lawson, Rebekah Joiner, John Ellis, *Joy*

Have you seen the movie *The Bucket List?* Two very simple questions are posed by Morgan Freeman during the film:

- Have you found joy in your life?
- Has your life brought joy to others?

Before we move on to the final section of this book, I would ask you to consider your legacy. What impact have you made or will you make on the lives of others? If you were being remembered tomorrow, what would your family say about you? What would be your friends' fondest memories of you? What imprint on our world or society will you have left?

It is not easy to truly consider this topic. It is very introspective and honestly, it is much easier to consider, and it really hits home in a more significant way, when a life-changing event takes place. When we lose a family member or close friend. When we receive news of a devastating illness.

How do you define joy? What joy have you found in your life? Are you able to make a list? What joy have you brought to others? When? How do you know?

Key Points

> Make Magic Happen

> Pay It Forward

> Toast for Change!

> Consider Your Legacy

CHAPTER 7

Outside Influences: The "OI" Factor

Core Focus Area in Definition of Your Personal Brand

Life Lessons

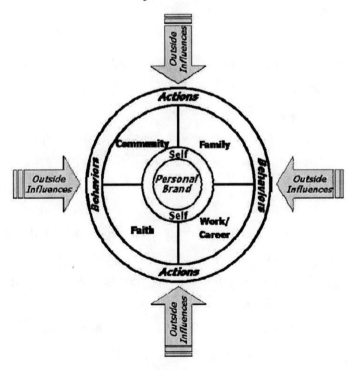

OUTSIDE INFLUENCES CAN MAKE OR BREAK YOUR PERSONAL BRAND

"Then what, What 'ya gonna' do, When the new wears off and the old shines through, And it ain't really love and ain't really lust, You ain't anyboby anybody's gonna trust, Then what, Where you gonna turn, When you can't turn back for the bridges you burned, And fate can't wait to kick you in the butt, Then what."
— Clay Walker, *Then What*

Let's start with the key message: Outside influences can be a positive *or* negative in the growth and development of your personal brand. Outside influences exist in every aspect of your life. Consider some of these questions pertaining to outside influences:

- How important is the advice, guidance and direction of others?
- Who do you trust? Why?
- What makes one person's perspective more appropriate or applicable to you and your life?
- How do you prioritize feedback, coaching and suggestions?
- What can you learn from your experiences with others outside of your sphere of influence?
- What do you observe in the behavior of others that you then apply to your life?
- How often do you allow societal influences to drive your decision-making process?

- Who has come into your life and had an influence on you, despite your lack of any sort of relationship with the individual?
- Do you allow gossip, slanted news media, and opinionated individuals to govern your thoughts and ideas?

You might be thinking that this chapter is set up to focus on the negative aspects of outside influences. My challenge to you is to view both sides — the positive and negative — of outside influences on your personal brand.

To use a true football analogy, winning teams are affected by outside influences constantly. Interpreting and executing plays on the field, making grades in the classroom, reading the "expert" news media and listening to talking heads, listening to fans and "high-dollar" supporters Sunday and Monday morning quarterbacking the team, understanding a competitor from game film — it is an amazing accomplishment to see a team go undefeated, win a national championship, win the Super Bowl, turn a losing season into a winning season or make accomplished athletes into successful business individuals.

Teams learn just as much from their own performance, as watching and learning from the decisions and actions of an opposing team. Many coaches "borrow" plays and line-ups from other teams after observing those teams on the field. At the same time, coaches are able to review decisions that did not work out for an opposing team, and ensure that their team does not follow suit. The coach's role as leader extends to both on and off the field. Often times these off-the-field distractions, including news media, professors, fans, supporters, premium-seat owners, and player families, influence the on-the-field team performance.

Our friends, family, co-workers, bosses, news media, talk shows, and much more offer a constant stream of marketing, communication, content and "noise" that influence our life decisions on a daily basis. Outside influences can be very tough to manage despite a strong will. Typically, emotions and personalities create complexity despite a focus on our relationship focus areas. Outside influences could be any of the following to name a few:

• Friends	• Bosses / managers	• Internet content
• Parents	• Peers	• Local / national TV
• Siblings	• Customers	• TV /radio talk shows
• Competitors	• Team members	• Politics
• Co-workers	• Extended family	• Societal trends

Let's turn to our personal lives. Recently, one of my close friends Catherine, received a phone call on a Sunday afternoon from her fiancé. He had decided to break-off their marriage, their relationship and of course, the ensuing wedding that was only two weeks away and did it over the phone with no further explanation. In a flurry to come to her rescue and be by her side in this tough time, her friends and family offered the "I know what you are going through" speech. And the "take time for yourself" speech. And even better, the "don't just jump into the next relationship as it will be a rebound" soliloquy.

The reality is that no one understands you like you. Nobody else truly knows your thoughts, feelings, pain or pleasure like you.

One of my pet peeves is when someone tells me that they know what I am feeling or going through or when I catch myself saying it to others. Even though a situation may be similar, it is not the same from one individual to another. These outside perspectives often frustrate more than they help an already difficult or even positive and happy situation.

As you evaluate the Self, Work / Career, Family, Faith and Community aspects of your personal brand, consider the outside influences that often impact the decisions you make in these relationship focus areas.

Outside influences can have a strong positive and / or negative impact on the strength of your personal brand. Think carefully about the integration of these influences in your decision-making process — choose wisely. It is especially difficult to sift through the actions, opinions and perceptions of others when going through an emotionally difficult situation. Do not allow the outside influences to drive, manage or lead your life. Take control and ensure that you balance the role of outside influences in the overall context of your personal brand.

CHAPTER 8

Your Personal Brand | Concluding Reflections

Brand-you. Your life-map. Who you are. The person behind your outward appearance. The impact you make on others. Your role in relationships. Your management of outside influences. Your desire to do the right thing. Your role as a leader. Faith's role in your life. Authentic leadership and your personal brand. Your legacy. Living out that personal brand every day.

You own your own personal brand. You own the decisions you make in life. You live with the results of life decisions. Your personal brand is a reflection of you. You have the opportunity to strengthen that brand by investing time in different relationship focus areas and through management of outside influences.

I love the concept of a personal brand. Of "Brand You." That our personal brand is represented every day. In the workplace. At home. With family, friends and strangers. In the community. And that we have the opportunity to increase or decrease its value over time through life decisions. We have the opportunity to live out our personal brand every day in all aspects of our life.

I decided to take a unique approach to the concept of personal branding in using my own life lessons and linking those to the personal brand concept. Obviously, no one person can do all of the things outlined in this book. What I have found is that if I take several key concepts and focus on those for a set period of time, I am able to successfully move forward in a positive life direction.

Get focused. Start today. Enjoy the journey. Make it happen! Live it out!!!

THE "LIO" MODEL

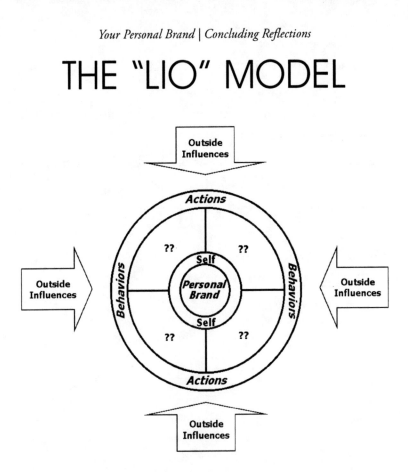

The *Live It Out (LIO)* personal brand model is simple and that is exactly what I love about it. It is a simple way to define and communicate what is important in our lives. It is a simple way to convey the importance of relationships in our lives. It is a simple way of grounding ourselves in the fact that we all maintain core values, beliefs, principles, experiences, and knowledge that are central to who we are as individuals.

I use the LIO model as part of a personal branding workshop. The workshop starts with participants completing a me-map, continues with the definition of core values and concludes with the creation of a personal LIO model containing four individually-selected core focus areas (e.g. Faith, Work / Career).

I have learned so much from the many stories shared by individuals as they describe why they have selected their four core focus areas — it is highly personal and at times, emotional.

The bottom line is that the model is simply a tool that enables the thought process around life priorities. It is another mechanism that assists in making life decisions. For more information about the LIO model or to order model kits, visit WWW.LIVEITOUTBRAND.COM.

Live it out every day!

About The Author

JUSTIN C. HONAMAN

Justin Honaman is a strategic business process and technology professional with a background in customer marketing and business intelligence.

As a dedicated community leader, Justin serves as a board member for several Atlanta-area business, leadership and philanthropic organizations, serves in multiple leadership roles at his church, and is involved as an advisory board member for several magazines.

In 2006, Justin released his first country music album, *Saturday in the South!* Recorded in Nashville, Justin is using his first album to raise money for Children's Healthcare of Atlanta (www.choa.org) through the Makin' Magic Happen Campaign for Kids.

Justin has been recognized by the Atlanta Business Chronicle as one of the "40-Under-40 Up-and-Comers" and was recognized as a "Top 25 Consumer Goods Industry Visionary / Rising Star" by Consumer Goods magazine.

Justin holds an Industrial and Systems Engineering degree from Georgia Tech and a Masters of Business Administration from Auburn University.

Learn more at
WWW.HONAMAN.COM

Coaches And Mentors

We all have coaches and mentors in life. People that encourage us. People that influence us in large and small ways. Thanks to the following individuals for their time, effort and concern — for making it happen with me!

Alex Clarke, *Coca-Cola Enterprises*

Paul Bierbusse, *Ernst & Young, LLP*

Rick Chirafisi, *Walt Disney World Parks & Resorts*

Greg Foster, *Noro-Moseley Partners*

Chan Gailey, *National Football League*

Jennifer Geiger, *Post Properties*

Rebecca Gregory, *North Point Community Church*

Jennifer Hale, *Organizational Impact*

Heidi Higgins, *Jan Smith Studios*

Dave King, *NASA*

Jim Marvel, *Coca-Cola Customer Business Solutions*

Jack Thompson, *Georgia Tech*

David Willis, *David and Rosetti, LLP*

Printed in the United States
151267LV00002B/1/P